INDISPENSABLE YOU!

7 Simple Things You Must Do To Keep Your Job Today (And Tomorrow)

Kim Andersen & Scott Pemberton

Writer: David Dee

Illustration: McNeel Studios

DARTNELL is a publisher serving the world of business with book manuals, newsletters and bulletins, and training materials for executives, managers, supervisors, salespeople, financial officials, personnel executives, and office employees. Dartnell also produces management and sales training videos and audiocassettes, publishes many useful business forms, and many of its materials and films are available in languages other than English. Dartnell, established in 1917, serves the world's business community. For details, catalogs, and product information, write:

THE DARTNELL CORPORATION

4660 N. RAVENSWOOD AVE
CHICAGO, IL 60640-4595, U.S.A.
OR PHONE (800) 621-5463 IN U.S. AND CANADA

CONTENTS   PAGE

CHAPTER TWO

CHAPTER THREE

CHAPTER FOUR

CHAPTER FIVE

CHAPTER SIX

CHAPTER SEVEN

#7. LET SELF-ASSESSMENT & SELF-DISCOVERY
CHART YOUR WAY TO *CAREER* SECURITY   117

PART II

THE CAREER SURVIVAL TOOL KIT   **141**

CHAPTER EIGHT

TOOL #1. MANAGING STRESS: KEEPING COOL AND CALM UNDER PRESSURE   **143**

CHAPTER NINE

CHAPTER TEN

INDEX   193

INTRODUCTION

Today's headlines tell the story:

"AT&T cuts 40,000 jobs"

"Sears Kills Catalog — 50,000 jobs, 113 stores eliminated"

"Boeing cuts 15,000 local jobs"

The good old days of enjoying a lifetime of work with one employer are long gone. Instead of long-term security and pension plans, companies today talk about the need to cut bureaucracy and shuffle people. In the 1990s, corporate downsizing, mass layoffs, and massive restructurings have become a way of life for most Americans.

The New York Times calls this the "new culture of permanent restructuring," a revolution that has resulted in the elimination of some 43 million U.S. jobs since 1980.

We can't promise you that you won't be laid off. The fact is, many competent, capable, loyal, enthusiastic, hardworking employees have been and will be let go from jobs they love.

We can't promise that you won't be forced to change jobs. Career consultants say the average employee entering the workforce will change careers three or four times during a lifetime and will change jobs up to 13 times.

We *can* promise you this: You do not have to remain powerless to these outside forces. That's where this book comes in.

As the editors of several business and communications-building newsletters for The Dartnell Corporation, we interview the experts and have our fingers on the pulse of the downsizing and reengineering trends affecting workers. What we've discovered is that the only job security that exists today is the job security you create for yourself. We've written this book to show you how to empower yourself with the skills that will make you the person *least likely* to ever be without a job during these volatile times.

Indispensable You! is *not* about learning how to program a computer or to search the job section for the position that will most likely get you hired. This book *is* about learning broader people skills that cut across job functions and strengthen teamwork, increase productivity, and ultimately, boost a company's bottom line.

Those are the skills every employer is looking for. Those are the skills that make you the *first* person employers want to hire and the *last* person they want to have let go. Because these powerful people skills are portable, they'll make you valuable and irreplaceable in any job or career. For that reason, being indispensable is the closest thing there is to a guarantee in these uncertain times.

We've divided *Indispensable You!* into two sections. In the first, you'll learn "The 7 Simple Things You *Must* Do to Keep Your Job Today (*And* Tomorrow)" — your action plan for career security. You'll learn how mastering these seven vital people skills will boost your career now and in the future:

The 7 Simple Things

#1: Treat *Everyone* Like Your Very Best Customer

#2: Develop Winning Ways with Coworkers

#3 Meet & *Exceed* Your Boss's Expectations

#4: Develop *Your* Powerful Communication Skills

#5: Build Better Relationships with Difficult People

#6: Motivate others to Give *Their* Best

#7: Let Self-Assessment and Self-Discovery Chart Your Way to *Career* Security (Listen to the best career counselor you know: You!)

You'll discover how every function ultimately provides service to an internal or external customer; develop a continuous learning mindset that prevents you from ever becoming obsolete; and gain the cooperation and respect of those with whom you work.

In the second section, we provide you three key tools that will help you put those people skills into action. In "The Career Survival Tool Kit," you'll learn tips and techniques for:

- **Managing stress.** In an era of cutbacks and downsizing, job stress is greater than ever. How do you cope with the pressure to do more in less time, with fewer resources? What are the most productive ways of handling the day-to-day stress of everchanging teammates and job descriptions?

- **Taking on technology.** Becoming complacent about technology will not only make you the 1990s equivalent of a dinosaur, it will make you more replaceable in today's job market. As your job description changes and you're expected to quickly adapt to new technology, the right mindset can make you more valuable to more employers.

- **Conquering time management.** When you're known as someone who has conquered time management, you increase your value to your current employer and build your long-term career security. More than ever, time is money, and the indispensable employees are those who show respect for the organization's time — and their own.

We hope that with this book, you'll be on your way to a future where you are no longer a victim to job trends, downsizing, cutbacks, and layoffs, a future where you are indispensable to *yourself* and totally in control of your own career destiny.

Kim Andersen & Scott Pemberton

A final note: Please *use* this book! Fill in the personal quizzes … check off the Quick Tips that you find most useful … add your responses to the "What would you do?" features … and jot down your comments in "Action Ideas." There's scientific proof that the messier you make a book, the more you're getting from it, so write away!

FOREWORD

As a career strategist, I've interviewed hundreds of job hunters and workers looking for new opportunities. What I've most often heard them say is this: "I wish I had the kinds of skills that most employers want. I don't think I do."

Here is the book they, and many others, have been waiting for. Outlined within these pages are the vital *portable* skills that are most sought by employers today — and that will continue to be highly valued for the rest of the 1990s and beyond. There is nothing that will be more important in the next ten years than the skills that can be used across jobs and industries.

As William Bridges, author of *Job Shift*, asserts, we are moving from an era in which we have individual jobs to an era in which we move from role to role. The key to mastery of new assignments, remaining state-of-the-art technically and in other ways, is the ongoing mastery of key skills. To have those key skills can boost you ahead of people with more experience, more education, more contacts, even better job-hunting skills.

Indispensable You! outlines the key skill sets needed to keep, and get, jobs. The book is a workbook, road map, and handy reference that can be used again and again as the need arises.

It's divided into two sections: the first describes what the authors call the 7 Simple Things, the key skill sets that make you employable today and can help keep you employable tomorrow. You can read them in order or go immediately to the one or two that you need help with immediately. The second part looks at three important skills every worker needs regardless of age, industry, job description or job title. Look at these carefully because they are the basic underpinnings of all successful careers.

At the end of each chapter you'll find a Career Survival Take-Away — a helpful review of the key points and action steps that can help you solve a problem, enhance a particular skill set, and make you indispensable almost immediately.

In an era in which books often seem to be written for people who would appear to have nothing else to do but read a lengthy, detailed discourse, this book is that surprising rarity: one that gives valuable information quickly and *succinctly*. You'll get the essence without having to wade through the process. But there is enough detail so you can put into practice the ideas and recommendations that solve problems. For example: haven't we heard every word in the language at least twice that describes "quality" or "good quality"? See Chapter 1, page 7 for a truly career-building description of quality — creating it, delivering it, and being recognized for it. Do you sometimes have trouble understanding what your boss does and why? See Chapter 3, page 43 for tips on analyzing your boss's style and what to do with your newfound knowledge. Is someone trying to sabotage your work with subtle — and not so subtle — put-downs? See Chapter 5, page 81.

What I like best, and believe you will too, is that the book is interactive. You can fill in the quizzes, make notes in the margins, refer often to information most useful to you. It's like having a personal career coach at hand as problems arise — but more compact and much less expensive. Using this resource won't guarantee that you'll be at the same organization for the next 20 years (Who can guarantee the organization *itself* will be around for the next 20 years?) but wherever you land and whoever you work for, this book can help you be seen as valuable to that organization. Plus, it can help you develop or refine those important *portable* skills that can help you step into a new position and become effective fast. So, don't delay starting on the road to indispensability right now!

Marilyn Moats Kennedy
Founder & Managing Partner
Career Strategies
Wilmette, Illinois

PART I

SEVEN SIMPLE THINGS YOU *MUST DO* TO KEEP YOUR JOB TODAY (*AND* TOMORROW)

CHAPTER ONE

Simple Thing #1:
TREAT *EVERYONE* LIKE YOUR VERY BEST CUSTOMER

"Make yourself necessary to somebody."

— RALPH WALDO EMERSON (1803-1882), PHILOSOPHER AND POET

INTRODUCTION

To his coworkers, Carlos sounded confused about who was on the phone. A caller from another department in the main building was asking Carlos to send over a skid of paper that was stored in the warehouse where Carlos worked.

"Mr. Barnes, our truck leaves in 25 minutes," Carlos told the caller. "So, I'll have the paper there by 3 p.m. Is that acceptable? Great. Thanks for calling."

When Carlos hung up the phone, his coworkers in the warehouse began to tease him. "Carlos, that was Ben. You play basketball with him every Wednesday night. What's this Mr. Barnes business?"

Carlos was not intimidated. "He's Ben on the court. Right now he's my *customer.*"

Carlos puts into action one of the key practices that will help make him indispensable in the workplace: He treats everyone who comes into contact with his work as though they are his most important customer.

Carlos realizes that his organization has two customers: those who purchase the product or service his company produces, the outside customers, and the other employees of the organization, the inside customers. He believes both deserve top-notch customer service.

"My job is to serve my customers in the building, so they can serve the customers who bring in money," Carlos explains. "If we don't do our part, that outside customer is going to do business somewhere else."

Treating everyone — whether they're across town or across the hall —like your best customer belongs at the top of your list of Simple Things You *Must* Do To Keep Your Job Today (*And* Tomorrow). It's the single most important thing you can do to make yourself irreplaceable.

Treating everyone like your best customer means offering *friendly, professional service.* That makes you someone your coworkers and customers enjoy doing business with. As a result, they will view you as dependable — and helpful. That makes you a valuable asset to your organization.

In this chapter, we look at a number of ways to improve the customer service you offer. When a technique serves outside customers, think of ways it can be adapted to help you serve internal customers as well. The more you think of coworkers and others as customers, the easier it becomes to serve them the way you serve your "paying" customers.

WHAT WOULD YOU DO?

'OUT OF SIGHT' SHOULDN'T MEAN 'OUT OF MIND'

*Y*our Midwest salesperson needs updates on product availability and shipping schedules for potential customers. She calls late in the day, just minutes before the office staff in New York is ready to leave for the day. Some of your coworkers let the line go unanswered so they can leave on time.

Many businesses have regional or even global branch offices. When you work with people from another branch office, it's easy to forget that you all work for the same organization and share the same goals. This long-distance operation doesn't dismiss the need for teamwork. In fact, it makes it even more important.

To achieve peak performance, coworkers on all levels and at all locations must cooperate. Your support of coworkers in the field, at another office, or in another department is key to your ultimate success.

If the home office staff is ignoring calls from the Midwest sales rep because she calls late in the day, that salesperson is working at a disadvantage — and so is the company. A competitor can provide potential customers with quick answers, while our salesperson must wait to obtain crucial data that may not come for days.

As you can see, lack of cooperation works against potential sales and profits. All callers to the office are entitled to be welcomed up until closing time. Conversely, the salesperson shouldn't expect lengthy reports when coworkers are leaving for the day.

Discuss the time problem with the salesperson — she may not be aware of the time zone difference and may not realize your inconvenience. Remember, when you serve her, you are indirectly serving your outside customers as well.

SMILES REALLY CAN SEND A POSITIVE MESSAGE

One of the most overused clichés in customer service is "put a smile in your voice" when you're on the phone with a customer.

Even though it's physically impossible for a voice to smile, putting a smile in your voice is just another way of saying, "Be sure to let customers know you're happy to hear from them."

Forcing a smile won't automatically send that message. In fact, if you are forcing yourself to smile, your tone may come across as phony, which defeats the whole purpose. However, many people who use the phone find that smiling before they pick up the phone helps them send an upbeat, positive message to their callers. Some receptionists, phone salespeople, and service reps keep a mirror by their phones to remind them to smile.

"I make a big effort to make all callers feel they are a priority by giving away a free smile," says customer service rep Blevyn Ferrell, Flint Equipment Co. "You may think that customers are on the phone and don't know whether I am smiling or not, but they do know. They can sense from my tone of voice that I am glad they called.

"Customers have come into the office and told me, 'You *do* have that smile I saw over the phone.' That's the biggest compliment they could ever give me," says Ferrell.

So go ahead, you can do it: Smile!

SERVICE WORKS FROM THE INSIDE OUT

The telephone is ringing in the service department. Lee is burdened with boxes of files, but still tries to answer it. Barb, who works in the accounting department, passes by. She sees Lee needs help, so she picks up the phone. Barb transfers the call to the right person. The caller is satisfied, and Lee is grateful.

Steve is a teller at a bank. After a morning of dealing with customers, he can finally do his paperwork. He sees a line of customers at Nan's window. Steve puts aside his paperwork and motions for the next customer to come over to his window.

Barb and Steve, though working in different companies with different needs, have learned a key secret: internal customer service — working cooperatively with coworkers to meet the shared goal of serving customers. They do what's best for the entire team, not just themselves.

In many organizations, different departments and their employees are literally each other's customers. Only when departments can satisfy the needs of others internally can the organization satisfy the external customer. By understanding your organization, its people, and all of its services, you will know who to contact if you, a customer, or business associate need something from another department. Here are other ways to improve internal customer service:

- **Return phone calls.** When a coworker calls, get back to him or her quickly. Another employee may need your expertise to serve a client. Also, you'll encourage coworkers to return your calls quickly if that's the treatment they get from you.

- **Share the information with others.** If you find a handy tip for performing a task, let others know about it. Share information about new products and services.

- **Help out.** Is that phone at the next desk ringing? Answer it. Does a coworker need files that you can locate? Retrieve them. Is a colleague trying to serve three customers simultaneously while two more wait? Offer a hand.

- **Communicate.** Too often interdepartmental communication is limited to managers, who don't do a lot of hands-on work. As a result, they might not be able to offer detailed information. Seek opportunities to get acquainted with coworkers from other departments. You might even ask your boss to help you plan ways to get depart-

ACTION IDEA

Make a chart with three headings:

• Department (for listing all your company's departments)

• Product (what those departments are responsible for)

• Contacts (who in that area you can call for help). Keep this list on hand.

Not only will you have a better understanding of where your job fits into the big picture, you'll also be able to identify how you can serve your coworkers — customers.

ments to interact better. Tell them what you do and ask what they do. Discuss common problems and potential solutions.

HOW DO YOU DEFINE QUALITY?

"It's a nice word and all, but what does it mean?" a frustrated customer service rep asked recently as she sipped coffee from her "Quality" coffee mug.

Ken Blanchard, author of *The One-Minute Manager* (William Morrow) and professor of leadership and organizational behavior at the University of Massachusetts at Amherst, says many managers and supervisors talk about the need for quality without explaining what it is and how it can be achieved.

Ask a customer what makes quality in a product or service, and the reply might be, "It's hard for me to describe it, but I know it when I see it." The customer is saying that quality is something that is perceived, or felt, as well as seen. A recent Gallup Poll asked 1,005 adults to measure quality in the companies they do business with. The top factors they cited were courteous or polite behavior, satisfied needs, promptness, and a satisfying past experience with the company. Quality, ultimately, is what the customer expects to receive and is satisfied with when that expectation is met.

"Quality is more than an attribute; quality is an attitude," says the narrator in the film *The Human Nature of Quality* (Dartnell).

Set your own quality goals. Forget the clichés and vague motivational posters. You can help bring meaning to your company's quality goals through your personal definition of quality. You may want to adopt the following goals for customer service excellence.

Each day, promise yourself:

1. To always maintain a professional manner and appearance.

2. To greet customers warmly and to always make them feel welcome and comfortable doing business with you and your organization.

3. To always be prompt, courteous, and friendly in serving customers.

4. To always adopt a problem-solving attitude when you handle complaints and inquiries.

5. To carefully assess each customer's needs and recommend specific products or services that will provide the highest level of satisfaction.

6. To find the right answers to all customer questions and to stay up-to-date on the products and services your company offers so you can pass the correct information on to your customers.

7. To be familiar with all organizational procedures and policies so you can handle every customer transaction with minimum error and delay.

ACTION IDEA

Jot down 3 of your own personal quality goals here. Reread them several times throughout the day to help keep you on course.

1. _____

   _____

   _____

   _____

   _____

   _____

2. _____

   _____

   _____

   _____

   _____

   _____

3. _____

   _____

   _____

   _____

   _____

   _____

   _____

8. To follow up on inquiries from customers and ensure their satisfaction.

9. To know your company's promotional campaigns and to support these efforts while you deal with customers.

10. To turn new customers into returning customers by providing the kind of service they expect and are entitled to.

WHO BENEFITS MOST FROM YOUR QUALITY PERFORMANCE?

The concepts of quality and customer satisfaction are sometimes hard to grasp. Some great breakthroughs have been made in measuring quality and tracking customer satisfaction, however, we can still have trouble understanding these concepts and keeping them in perspective.

Several ideas can help you remember the importance of delivering quality work and service. They can help make quality and tracking customer satisfaction "real."

- Your customer is anyone who receives your work. The concept of "customer" is not limited to the end user of your organization's products or services. If a customer is anyone who receives your work, then that means you probably have quite a few customers — both outside and inside your organization.

  External customers are those who buy and use your organization's products and services. Internal customers work next to you or in other departments. In short, your customers consist of anyone your work touches. Identify them, and serve them to the best of your ability.

- The quality of your work directly affects your customers' work or personal lives. Your customers count on you to deliver quality work and service because they can't do their best unless you do yours. What happens when you deliver quality to your customers? What happens when you don't?

- Customers seek you out or avoid you based on the quality of your work. Your success is determined by your customer's perception of the quality of your work and service. This happens in the marketplace all the time. Organizations that deliver quality products and services — and satisfy their customers — succeed because their customers come back for more. The same is true inside your organization. When you satisfy internal customers, you win their support and give yourself the opportunity to succeed in your job and your career. Deliver less than the best, and your internal customers — your coworkers — won't give you the support you need to succeed.

- The person who benefits most from your excellent work and quality service is *you*. Beyond the professional success you'll earn at work when you deliver quality to your customers are the greater rewards of personal satisfaction and high self-esteem. And these aren't rewards you have to wait for. You get them immediately every time you deliver the best, whether internally or externally.

Remember the saying, "You are what you do"? What kind of person do your customers say you are? Are you one that delivers quality? And, maybe more important, when you finish your own work and look back on what you've accomplished at the end of a day, what kind of person can you say you are?

So, who benefits most from a quality performance? In short, you do. Go ahead — work well and enjoy!

SHARE INFORMATION WITH INSIDE CUSTOMERS

No one would dispute the importance of good communication with your company's customers. But what about the importance of communicating with your coworkers — those "customers" you serve within your organization? Information sharing can be a powerful tool to aid colleagues, helping them to do their jobs more easily with fewer errors in less time. It can also nurture a team approach to achieving a shared goal: satisfying the outside customer.

Use the following approaches to develop your information-sharing habit:

- **Capitalize on electronic mail.** If you have access to e-mail, send messages to one or more individuals at the same time. In less than five minutes, you can tell an entire network what you learned by talking to an important customer, or how you solved a problem. For example, you may identify which of several items is the most popular with customers, when complaints are most likely and from which people, and which suppliers respond to requests on time.

- **Provide tips on job forms.** A California manufacturing firm encourages all those associated with a special job to write comments that will help everyone involved. Those in the warehouse, plant floor, shipping, and customer service share information about the customer, parts needed, problems encountered, and shipping arrangements. Group involvement through shared information leads to increased quality productivity and service.

- **Share articles of interest.** Route articles you think coworkers might like to read. Then everyone can benefit from your research. In some companies, articles, newsletters, announcements, and brochures are passed around and then filed for reference.

- **Use staff meetings.** Come to meetings with materials you have obtained at a conference or trade show. Take the time before the meeting to highlight or underline what you think is of most impor-

ACTION IDEA

To meet you customers'
expectations, you must
understand what your
customers want. Take
a few minutes to ask
yourself these
questions:

1. What do customers
want from me and from
my company?

2. How do support
areas — like billing and
shipping — work to
serve my customers?
How can I work in har-
mony with other areas
so we can better serve
customers?

3. What are the
details — the little
things — that make a
big difference in my
customers' satisfaction?

tance. Then briefly indicate what you will be circulating and why you feel it's worth reading.

- **Broadcast via the department bulletin board.** Have you ever come across suggestions on how to do a job more effectively? If company policy allows, post the item. The posting habit is a simple, cost-effective way to distribute information — especially if people are in the habit of checking the board.

- **Share personal experiences.** Let others learn from your victories and your mistakes. Take a moment after a successful interaction with a supplier to let a coworker know what you learned. By sharing, you not only let others profit from what you have learned, but they might share related information, too.

CUSTOMERS EXPECT *YOU* TO MAKE YOUR BUSINESS WORK FOR THEM

Customers believe there is no distinction between you and your company. If you treat them well, your company has treated them well. Thus, the cardinal rule in customer service that everyone on your team should follow is: *You are the company.*

"Customers don't know how things get done behind doors marked EMPLOYEES ONLY," say Kristin Anderson and Ron Zemke in *Delivering Knock Your Socks Off Service* (AMACOM Books). "They don't know your areas of responsibility, your job description, or what you personally can and cannot do for them. And they don't care. To customers, those things are *your* business, not theirs."

How do you put the "You are the company" rule into action? Start by choosing your language carefully. Use *I* instead of *they* or *we*. Using *I* shows that you understand and accept that the company begins and ends with you," say Anderson and Zemke.

Next, get to know your organization inside and out. "Customers expect you to make the organization work for them," say the authors. "They expect you to understand the big picture and to be able to answer their questions, solve their problems, and refer them to just the right people for just the right things."

Finally, constantly review what customers need and how you can serve them better. "In your hands is the power to make that contact magical," explain the authors. "In your hands is the power to keep customers coming back."

10 TRAITS FOR TOP-OF-THE-LINE CUSTOMER SERVICE

Customer service involves everyone. But is everyone well-suited for serving customers? The H.R. Chally Group, a research firm, defined 10 characteristics of those who are most successful helping customers. How do you measure up?

1. They are optimistic and enthusiastic. Employees with these characteristics expect positive results and will "hang in there" during tough times. They find that their optimism is a self-fulfilling prophecy that spreads to coworkers and customers.

2. They have a positive mental attitude. People with a positive attitude tend to be solution-oriented. Negative events are regarded as valuable learning experiences.

3. They are constructively competitive. Competitive individuals enjoy competing with others ("I'll be the best in the department!"), but they know how to accept defeat. And their competitive spirit helps motivate them to do better.

4. They are people-oriented. Customer service involves two persons — you and a customer. You have to enjoy interaction to provide superior service.

5. They have inquiring minds. People with inquiring minds like to solve problems. They define problems and select pertinent information for developing solutions. Their curiosity often leads to innovative improvements that benefit others.

6. They are organized. Well-organized people strive for accurate information because they need to perform tasks correctly to feel comfortable. When these people make a promise, the customer — whether internal or external — can feel assured the person will deliver.

7. They consider others. They put their own egos and concerns aside to ensure that others are happy.

8. They can make decisions. Those with this skill know how to gather all the information they need before making a decision. They know how to make decisions that are compatible with their companies' overall goals.

9. They are communicators. They have developed their skills to make points in a clear, logical, and interesting manner. These folks know how to focus on what a customer is saying and to ask questions. This kind of people person can quickly respond to others' questions and needs.

10. They know their product or service well. Strong people skills are important but so is a thorough knowledge of company products or services. Those who serve customers most effectively know how to show customers how their needs can be met by their companies or departments.

MISSING NO MORE: HOW TO RECAPTURE LOST CUSTOMERS

Customer loyalty can never be taken for granted particularly when a company mistake has damaged a formerly good relationship. "That's when you need excellent 'recovery skills' that will help recapture the customer's goodwill," says Lisa Ford, president of The Ford Group, Inc., of Atlanta, Georgia.

When a mistake is made, Ford advises, apologize sincerely. "This sounds basic," she admits, "but I hear a lot of complaints from customers about apologies that aren't really apologies," Ford says. Your voice, facial expression, and eye contact should show that you really regret the customer's difficulties.

Then use these steps to recapture the customer's loyalty:

- Fix the problem, not the blame. "Customers are only concerned with having the problem fixed," Ford emphasizes. "They're not interested in who did what, or why it happened. They want action that will put things right."

- Use extras to compensate for the inconvenience. "Just fixing the problem isn't enough to win back the trust and loyalty of the customer," Ford says. "The way the customer looks at it, things should have been done right the first time around. And because they weren't, the customer has spent time, energy, and perhaps even money dealing with the problem."

  Your company may offer compensation as a matter of policy. Ford cites a dental office that offers movie passes or $10.00 off the bill for clients who have had to wait for their appointments. (Follow any such policy with enthusiasm, however. The tellers at one bank sparked a flurry of new service complaints by very grudgingly handing out the $5 bills promised to all customers who had to wait in line longer than five minutes.)

  Even if your company doesn't provide such compensation, Ford says, you can help make amends for the customer's inconvenience. Call the customer about a week after the problem has been resolved. Repeat your apology for the inconvenience, ask if the customer is satisfied, and thank him or her for allowing you to solve the problem. Then, follow up this call with a handwritten note thanking the customer for his or her patience. Invite the customer to contact you personally with any questions or concerns.

- Always ask for repeat business. "Be very direct about this," Ford advises. "When you call the customer to see if he or she is satisfied with the resolution, you could end by saying, 'We hope you'll continue to do business with us. Based on how we handled this problem, will you?'"

IT TAKES MORE THAN AN APOLOGY TO WIN BACK CUSTOMERS

What makes customers happy *after* a problem has occurred?

Linda Cooper, of the consulting firm Cooper & Associates in Evanston, Illinois, says customers expect more than an apology and a correction. Cooper recently surveyed bank retail customers and asked what they expect when a problem occurs. Their top 10 service expectations are:

1. Being called back when promised.

2. Being told how a problem happened.

3. Knowing whom to contact with a problem.

4. Being contacted when a problem has been resolved.

5. Being allowed to talk with someone in authority.

6. Being told how long it will take to fix a problem.

7. Getting alternatives if a problem cannot be resolved.

8. Being treated like a person, not an account number.

9. Being told about ways to prevent a future problem.

10. Receiving progress reports if a problem can't be resolved immediately.

The message is clear: You're job isn't completed when you've corrected a customer's problem. Customers expect (and deserve) some follow up.

DELIVER SURPRISINGLY SUPERIOR SERVICE

There it was, splashed across the television screen in big bold letters: **"WHY IS SERVICE SO BAD?"**

The accompanying news story examined many facets of service in the United States and included personal interviews with a number of customers, asking them to rate the quality of service in general. The verdict was not good for customer service reps. Almost unanimously, customers said "service is not what it used to be" and shared personal horror stories of poor treatment by service reps. No one, from the corner newsboy to the president of an airline, was spared criticism for not treating customers as well as they ought to be treated.

What can be done to change the public's perception about customer service? Many of the solutions are beyond the control of the average employee. But one solution you can put into action is this: Surprise your customers by offering them the kind of service they believe no longer exists! Here are three ways you can achieve this simple personal goal:

- Surprise customers by always being courteous. Treat customers the way you like to be treated when you're the customer. Kevin Orchard, who handles billing claims for an HMO, says, "At the end of the day, if I'm not careful, I'm not as courteous and patient with callers as I'd like to be." So he pretends that each call is actually the

ACTION IDEA

Make yourself indispensable to your organization by showing an interest in preventing future problems. Be proactive in suggesting to management changes that you think will avert the kinds of problems or concerns that damage customer loyalty. Watch for trends. Let's say you've taken a few calls from confused customers about an item in your company's mail order catalog. They've ordered the merchandise, only to discover that the color was not as depicted in the catalog. Track these calls, and make a positive suggestion to the appropriate person. It may be something like, "Perhaps we need to alter the description to depict this item more accurately in the catalog."

first call of the day. "It's a little game I play to help me give each customer all the energy and enthusiasm I gave the first call that morning," he says.

• Surprise customers by doing more than they ask for. When Karla Gleason returned a spoiled item to the grocery store, the manager not only apologized and gave her a replacement, but he also refunded the $15 she had spent that day on her groceries.

Karla used that experience at her job at an airline reservation desk. "Obviously I can't be giving away flights," she says. "But I try to make each customer interaction special, something the customer will remember." For example, during the holidays, she stayed 40 minutes past her shift to find a seat for a homebound college student whose seat had been bumped by another airline.

• Surprise customers by taking pride in your work. While Valerie Alverez was in line at a fast-food restaurant, a customer grumbled about the slow service and said, "I guess that's all you can expect when people are getting paid only four bucks an hour." Valerie went back to her own customer service job with a renewed sense of commitment. "It's true that those of us in service are notoriously underpaid," she says. "But that's no excuse for shortchanging the service we provide customers."

Surprise customers who have come to expect the worst by always being professional in your dress and manner. Speak of your work with a sense of pride. Show a positive, pleasant attitude. Give customers a friendly smile, call them by name, and do everything possible to make their experience with your company a pleasant one.

HAVE YOU CALLED THESE CUSTOMERS LATELY?

Many organizations call their new customers to say, "Thanks for choosing us." But new customers aren't the only customers you could be calling. Lloyd Finch, in *Telephone Courtesy & Customer Service* (Crisp Publications), suggests making a point of calling these customers as well:

• The irate customer. This customer may be the last person you feel like speaking with right now. But whether the cause of the customer's complaint was legitimate or questionable, a follow-up call is a good way to smooth over relations.

• The "nothing went right" customer. Sometimes, despite every effort, nothing goes right. Once all the problems have been corrected, call the customer to be sure everything is now satisfactory. And don't forget to ask if there's anything more you can do.

• The regular customer. Don't take your regular customers for granted. Keep in touch with them. An occasional friendly follow-up call tells customers, "We care about you."

HOLD THE PHONE! TRY A NOTE INSTEAD

It never hurts to call your customers, but those who know you only over the telephone will take notice when they receive a thank-you or other personal note in the mail. Writing notes is a great way to say thanks to your customers. Try these:

- "Thank you for your confidence in me. It was my pleasure to be of service to you."
- "It is my business to see that you continue to be satisfied. Please do not hesitate to call whenever I can be of further service to you."
- "You can be assured that (name your company) and I will do everything possible to . . ."
- "May I take a moment to express my sincere thanks for ... ."

Don't hesitate to write; even an informal note will do.

HOW TO GENERATE POSITIVE 'WORD-OF-MOUTH'

"You would have thought I committed some heinous crime or something."

That's how Odella Martin describes the reaction she got from friends when she told them she had begun working for the customer service department of a local retail chain. The problem, Martin learned, was that a friend of a friend had a horrible experience returning defective merchandise to that particular store. The group of friends all agreed never to do business with the store again.

Martin assured her friends that she wouldn't work at the company if she was expected to carry out any such atrocities. And her friends finally forgave her for taking the job. But Martin learned a valuable lesson: Companies should never underestimate the value of bad word-of-mouth advertising.

Consultant Jerry R. Wilson agrees. "Every company has a reputation or image. Every day, people talk about the company, its products, and its services. This talk adds a little or subtracts a little from that reputation," he says. Unfortunately, customers talk most about bad experiences. "For every three people willing to tell a positive story about your company, there are 33 others who will tell horror stories," he estimates.

The problem, says Wilson, is not that dissatisfied customers complain, but that they don't take their complaints to the owner or the manager: "They complain to their families, friends, and coworkers." And customers don't tell others about average service. They will, however, tell others about great service, he says. "Ask a satisfied customer about how he likes a supplier and he will say, 'Oh, he's OK.' Ask the same of an enthusiastic customer and his reaction will be something like, 'That place is the greatest. They really give you extra attention and service. Let me tell you what they did for me last week.'"

ACTION IDEA

Prepare three or four different notes to keep as templates. Although each customer note you write will be personalized, the templates provide you with a starting point. Without the formidable task of writing new letters each time, you'll be inclined to write more notes. And the templates assure that you include everything you want to say in each letter.

The way to generate positive word-of-mouth about your company is to "blow customers away by exceeding their every expectation," says Wilson. In his book, *Word-of-Mouth Marketing* (John Wiley & Sons), Wilson identifies four qualities you should cultivate to help generate positive word-of-mouth about your organization:

- Friendliness. "This is not the 'Have a nice day' automatic slogans that slip meaninglessly out of the mouth, but genuine friendliness," he says.

- Helpfulness. "This involves cultivating a sincere desire to help people make their buying decisions."

- Unflappability. Don't take customer complaints personally.

- Gamesmanship. "View serving others as a game without losers. The object is to win satisfaction. Ask yourself, 'How much do I have to do to win this game?' The only way for me to win is to absolutely convince you that I am a genuinely concerned, service-oriented person."

NOW A PAUSE . . . FOR SOME INSPIRATIONAL THOUGHTS

"It's not good enough to be just a good salesperson, secretary, or manager," says Byrd Baggett. "We must strive to be the best at what we do. We must remember we are only one bad experience away from losing any customer. That is why providing excellent service is so important," he says. To help you achieve that goal, Baggett has written 236 inspirational thoughts and suggestions and compiled them in a book, *Satisfaction Guaranteed* (Rutledge Hill Press). Here is a sampling of his ideas:

- "View customers as people, not statistics."

- "No matter how large your company, treat customers as if your survival depends on them. It does."

- "Customers want solutions, not excuses."

- "Do simple things in an exceptional way."

- "Sales get customers; service keeps them."

- "Customer service is either good or bad. There is no in-between."

CUSTOMER COMPLAINTS? NO PROBLEM!

Every company has some unhappy customers, but handling them successfully need not be a complicated process. Most complaints can be addressed with these five key steps:

1. Prepare.

a. Check your body posture. Even when the customer has no visual contact with you, body language says plenty about your attitude.

Uncrossed limbs and erect posture mean you are attentive and ready to listen to customers.

b. Have paper and pen close at hand. Taking notes keeps you focused on the content of the message and serves as a good written record of the conversation.

c. Clear your mind. Resist the tendency to slip into "automatic." One customer service rep says she stays fresh by envisioning a blackboard in her mind. She simply erases it after each call and begins all calls with a clean slate.

2. Listen Rationally.

a. Listen without interrupting. Even if a caller is complaining loudly, you'll need to hear everything he or she says. Don't allow other thoughts to prevent you from focusing on the customer's concern.

b. Provide feedback. In person, use gestures and facial expressions to show that you are carefully listening. On the phone, be sure to use phrases such as "Yes," "I understand," and "What happened next?"

3. Ask Questions.

Your caller needs to know you're both on the same team. To do this:

a. Use the customer's name during the conversation.

b. Indicate that you have taken notes. Say: "I'm writing some notes so I'll understand exactly what happened."

c. Ask questions to clarify your understanding.

4. Create the Solution.

a. Ask what the customer wants. Grant the request, if you can. If not, work out a solution you both agree on.

b. Speak in positives. Don't say: "We can't do anything until next Tuesday." Instead, say: "I'd be happy to schedule a service call for Tuesday."

5. Confirm and Close.

a. Review your agreement. Say: "I want to be sure we're both clear about what I'm going to do."

Then do it! It's imperative that you take precisely the action you've promised. Without that, you'll lose all the credibility and confidence you've worked so hard to gain with your customers.

FOLLOW THESE '10 SERVICE COMMANDMENTS' *RELIGIOUSLY*

There's more to handling a customer's problem than just correcting it. Failure to follow up, for example, may negate the goodwill you've generated by handling the problem promptly and efficiently. The next time you're handling a complaint or other problem, review these 10 questions to be sure you're covering all the bases. It is based on the First National Bank of Chicago's "10 Customer Service Commandments":

1. Do I call customers back when promised?

2. When a customer has a problem, do I clearly explain the cause of the difficulty?

3. Do I make sure callers know the names and numbers of the people they should speak with about their problem?

4. Do I promptly let customers know when problems have been corrected?

5. Do I allow unhappy customers to speak to someone in authority when they ask?

6. Do I give customers an idea of how long it will take to resolve a problem?

7. Do I offer useful alternatives if the problem cannot be resolved exactly as customers would like?

8. Do I treat customers like people — not numbers?

9. Do I tell customers how they may avoid future problems?

10. Do I provide progress reports to customers if problems can't be solved immediately?

When you've answered "yes" to all of these questions, you can feel relatively sure you are meeting customers' needs when they have complaints or problems. Remember, customers feel better about the outcome if you treat them like partners in the problem-solving process. That means keeping the lines of communication open.

QUICK TIPS

- **Provide probing dialogue.** When you need information from customers but they are quiet or uncooperative, try open-ended questions like, "Tell me more about the trouble you had with … ?" and "You were expecting delivery at 2 o'clock but … ?"

- **No more "I don't knows."** Never tell customers, "I don't know." Instead, say, "That's a good question. Let me find out." Then find out the answer and respond quickly.

- **Know thy customer!** It's best to tailor the service you provide by knowing what is important to customers. Don't guess. Instead, ask. Customers will be flattered and pleased that you are so determined to meet their unique needs.

- **Cater to customer needs.** About 68 percent of customers who stop doing business with a company say they did so because the company was indifferent to their needs, reports *Quality at Work* (Crisp). Show your customers you care.

- **Courtesy quickie.** "May I," "Thank you," and "Please." Use these phrases and you'll always be on the right road to customer courtesy.

- **Don't be caught off guard.** When a customer returns a call, be prepared. Don't say, "Oh, yes, Miss Blake. Now what was it I was calling you about? Let me see, I have that file here somewhere … ." Instead: "Miss Blake, thank you for taking the time to call me back. I have a question regarding … ." Write yourself notes when you leave messages so you quickly know what the callback is all about.

QUIZ

Customers Gauge Quality by Service You Provide

The person your customers have contact with is the person who holds the key to quality in their eyes. Your customers' entire perception of your company is based on their experience with *you*. So what can you do to be sure you're providing quality service? The following quiz can help. The questions are based on the results of a recent Gallup Poll in which 1,005 respondents were asked to measure the quality of the companies they do business with. Answer each question, then score yourself below. How often do you:

	ALWAYS	SOMETIMES	NEVER
1. Go the extra mile to satisfy customers' needs?	❐	❐	❐
2. Provide courteous, polite service?	❐	❐	❐
3. Sound alert on the phone?	❐	❐	❐
4. Double-check your accuracy?	❐	❐	❐
5. Answer calls promptly?	❐	❐	❐
6. Show that you "know your stuff" by answering questions correctly?	❐	❐	❐
7. Listen closely to callers?	❐	❐	❐
8. Treat customers as individuals?	❐	❐	❐
9. Take responsibility for mistakes?	❐	❐	❐
10. Let callers know that you appreciate their business?	❐	❐	❐
TOTALS	____	____	____

Your score: Allow yourself 10 points for every statement you responded to with *always*; five for every *sometimes*; and no points for each *never*. A score of 80–100 is excellent; a score of 60–80 is good; while less than 65 means you could do more to give customers the quality service they expect and deserve. Remember, customers put the responsibility for quality squarely on your shoulders. Let them know that you take that responsibility seriously!

YOUR CAREER SURVIVAL TAKE-AWAY

The 1st simple thing you _must_ do to keep your job today (_and_ tomorrow)

Treat everyone _like your best customer_

It's no secret: Your value to your organization increases in direct correlation to how you help increase your company's bottom line. When you provide superior service to your customers, your customers reward you and your organization with their return business. This means that the happier you make customers and the more they return, the more irreplaceable you are to your company.

Effective customer service skills are the tools that help you add value to your position. Indispensable employees know that outside customers aren't their only customers. They recognize the importance of providing their coworkers (or inside customers) the same top-notch service they offer other customers. Serving inside customers effectively makes the workplace more enjoyable and improves communication and productivity. The result: better service and a better bottom line for your organization.

WHAT YOU CAN DO

- **Learn where you fit in your organization.** Who are your customers inside your company? Who are the customers you serve outside?

- **Even if you don't serve customers directly, become familiar with skills that create friendly, professional, dependable customer service.**

- **Answering the phone promptly and responding quickly to requests shows others you are dependable.** Good speaking and listening skills show that you are interested in what others have to say.

- **Create a definition of quality service that has meaning for you.** Set personal service goals and strive to attain them.

- **Learn to adapt basic customer service skills to the way you treat the customer who works alongside you — your coworker.**

CHAPTER TWO

Simple Thing #2:
DEVELOP WINNING WAYS WITH COWORKERS

"Kindness is the oil that takes the friction out of life."

— ANN LANDERS (1918 -), NEWSPAPER COLUMNIST

INTRODUCTION

No doubt about it: Your experience in practical areas such as computers, foreign languages, writing, and public speaking will help keep you employed in these volatile times. But the skill that makes you most indispensable in the eyes of employers is the skill your parents began teaching you at an early age: *the ability to get along with others.*

According to a recent survey of 124 companies in 34 industries, bosses rate being a team player as the number 1 value they look for in their workers. The study, conducted by Challenger, Gray & Christmas Inc., found that nearly 40 percent of the bosses and managers surveyed ranked team player as top among seven desirable work traits. Moreover, 80 percent chose it as either first, second, or third.

So it should come as no surprise to job applicants who find that their potential employer is just as interested in their hobbies and other interests as they are in their technical skills. The employer is trying to discover if the potential employee is someone who will fit in, who will get along well with her coworkers and supervisor, and who will make the workplace a more enjoyable place.

Developing winning ways with coworkers is the second Simple Things You *Must* Do to Keep Your Job Today (*And* Tomorrow), and it is more important today than at any other time in the workplace. In years gone by, an employee may have worked side-by-side with the same coworkers for 20 or 30 years. But today that's all changed, due to downsizing and career-minded people moving from one job to another with greater frequency. Even in more stable work environments, where work team assignments change, or departments undergo restructuring, work partners are constantly changing. As a result, working well with a new group of people quickly and efficiently has become an increasingly important benchmark of employability.

Whether you stay where you are today, or you find yourself changing jobs, there's no better way to take charge of your career than to strengthen your "getting along" skills. With this valuable people skill, you win the support and cooperation of your coworkers and make it easier to meet your goals and the goals of your team and department. Besides, the workplace is much more pleasant when there's an atmosphere of mutual respect and goodwill. That alone is reason enough to make getting along a priority as you look for ways to bulletproof your career.

WHAT WOULD YOU DO?

ESCAPING THE GABFEST

You're facing a heavy deadline when you see a coworker heading your way. You're about to become entangled in an office gabfest you don't have time for.

When you have higher priorities and your visitor is persistent, be tenacious, yet polite. Here are some suggestions to help you avoid an extended conversation:

- **Stress urgency.** Explain how busy you are and that you'd like to talk later. Maybe you can suggest getting together for lunch. Or offer the person three minutes of your time — no more. You might even try picking up your phone, indicating that you must make a telephone call. Most likely, your visitor will get the message.

- **Stand up.** Remain standing as the intruder talks. Don't offer a chair. Most conversations become much shorter in a less relaxed atmosphere.

- **Get going.** Take a piece of paper or folder off your desk. Slowly move away, muttering something about "taking the report to Accounting" — or some other believable task.

DO YOU ACT LIKE YOU'RE PART OF A GREAT TEAM?

Have you ever felt isolated from your coworkers, as if you didn't belong? You can change that feeling. Research shows that people who view themselves as team members are much more interested in working with colleagues.

Here are some tips on how to join the lineup:

- **Think like a team member.** A chain is only as strong as its weakest link. Your company is only as good as you are.

- **Be an active teammate.** Share your work goals with coworkers and ask them to help. Then, be sure to help them achieve their goals.

- **Take responsibility.** When a problem comes up, solve it as if it were yours. Don't look for scapegoats. That will alienate your colleagues.

- **Know that you represent the team.** You are the company for customers or suppliers you talk with. You're important!

CAN COWORKERS BE FRIENDS?

In the 1950s, Ella Cook and Loretta Davis worked one desk apart in the tiny administrative office of an Iowa hospital. They spent their lunch hours together sharing office gossip and complaining about the hospital cafeteria food. Today, living at opposite ends of the country, their days working together in a crowded office are long over, but their friendship has endured.

"When you go to work for a company, you hear all about the insurance, the vacation days, all those wonderful benefits," says Davis. "But the greatest benefit of all is the opportunity you have to make some wonderful friends."

Most of us admit we like having friends but, for a variety of reasons, true friendship is surprisingly rare. Pollster Daniel Yankelovich found that seven out of 10 Americans admit to having many acquaintances but few close friends. Most feel this leaves a serious void in their lives. And, as Americans spend more time making a living and less making friends, this void appears likely to grow.

Should you try to build deeper, more meaningful friendships at work? "People often are leery of making friends at work," observes Frank McBride, a sociologist who has studied business friendships. "They know that, by their very nature, friendships in the office can be much more transitory than other relationships."

Many dynamics exist in the workplace. Understandably, people fear that another person is a friend out of convenience or that someone they trust may use the friendship for some gain in the office. "People should not close themselves off to the possibility of making a true friend at work," suggests McBride. "They just must be prepared to work harder at the relationship because the workplace offers so many obstacles."

How can you make successful friendships at work? One way is to communicate openly about potential obstacles. Secretary Joyce Rose is best friends with Billi McCormack, whose promotion recently made her secretary to the company president.

"We had a lot to talk about when Billi got that promotion," admits Rose. "I brought up being a little jealous because this put her far ahead of me pay-wise. And Billi needed to feel assured I wasn't going to ask any special favors now that I had an 'in' in the president's office. By talking about it, we were able to go on with our lives and friendship without worrying that those problems would crop up someday."

Keeping business and friendship separate also helps. Try to establish clear boundaries between the two. Keep personal issues out of your business-related discussions.

The bottom line: Exercise a little caution, and there's no reason to deny yourself the enjoyment of having a true friend at work. You'll gain more pleasure in your personal life and have more satisfaction on the job.

HELPING A COWORKER THROUGH A PERSONAL CRISIS

When a coworker suffers a personal misfortune, there's a natural urge to sympathize. Though it's easy to feel compassion, it can be hard to convey. You can help in these ways:

- Listen carefully. Let your coworker feel comfortable expressing his feelings. Avoid taking sides in a professional dispute. Just be an attentive listener.

- Help him to accept reality. It can seem comforting to minimize or deny the impact of the trouble, but avoid that tendency. Instead, try to provide a helpful perspective.

- Focus on strengths. At times of loss, people's self-confidence often flags under stress. Help your coworker keep perspective by reminding him of past achievements.

- Offer to help. Perhaps your supervisor will let you assist your friend so she can leave a few minutes early. Ask your coworker what he thinks would help most.

- Set aside time for your coworker. Make sure he knows you're available during his difficult period.

HOW TO BE 'ON THE JOB' WHEN COWORKERS ARE OFF

When employees are home sick or on vacation, everyone else is expected to pitch in and make sure business goes on as usual. OfficeTeam's temporary staffing specialists offer these recommendations:

- Take advantage of the opportunity. Show that you are a willing team player. Volunteer to pick up the slack and handle the responsibilities of coworkers who are not at work.

- Broaden your experience. Find out if your company will be hiring temporary or contract help to share the workload. If so, point out your supervisory skills and offer to oversee temporary employees. Be prepared to explain why you think your supervisory contributions will benefit the company.

THANKS WORK MAGIC

Here are two syllables guaranteed to work wonders: "Thank you." It is a simple, inexpensive phrase to use, but quite often is ignored or used without feeling. However, it is one of the most effective human relations tools around. Here are some ways to maximize the use of this magic phrase:

- Make it sincere. People often say "thank you" out of reflex. If you say it with some feeling, it becomes an all new phrase.

ACTION IDEA

Each day, jot down the names of three people who deserve your thanks today.

1. _____
2. _____
3. _____

Now list something specific you can thank each person for.

1. _____
2. _____
3. _____

Check each name off after you've thanked the person. Don't let a day end without checking off all three.

- Don't mumble. Don't act as if you are ashamed of saying "thank you." That only lessens its value.

- Give thanks by name. If several people are involved, don't just say "Thanks, everyone." Name them to personalize the gesture.

- Look at the people you thank. If they're worth being thanked, they're worth being looked at.

- Make it specific. A "Thanks for everything" is not nearly as meaningful as "Thank you for helping me compile the figures on my sales report, Penny. They were crucial to my presentation's success."

- Thank people when they least expect it. Thanks are even more powerful when they are least expected. Surprise people with your appreciation.

- Put it in writing. A short handwritten note might take time, but it's effort well-spent. Better yet, drop a note to a coworker's boss when special appreciation is in order.

TEAMWORK *Is* FUN AND GAMES

Humor can be a team-building tool when it provides a shared experience of laughter, says Jeff Justice of Corporate Comedy in Atlanta. "Appropriate humor can bond people and make them feel included in the group," says Justice. "Using sarcasm to put people down is not using humor appropriately, of course. But poking fun at the absurdity of a particular situation at work helps bring people together. It can ease that feeling of being the only one who's stressed out. Shared moments of humor can be a way of emphasizing, 'We're all in this crazy situation together, so let's make the most of it.'"

Here are Justice's tips for productive use of humor:

- Don't be afraid to poke fun at yourself. "I get some horrified responses when I recommend this," notes Justice. "The common reaction is, 'But people won't take me seriously if I make fun of myself!' But the opposite is true. They'll think you must be very confident in who you are and what you do. Politicians know this. Remember, Ronald Reagan, who probably won reelection because of his own ability to poke fun at his age: 'I am not going to make age an issue. I refuse to exploit for political gain my opponent's [Walter Mondale] youth and inexperience.'"

Take the task seriously — and yourself lightly. Win people over with self-deprecating humor such as, "I know you all picked me to lead this project because I know less than anyone here." You can even use your own mistakes as the basis for humor: "Let's not do what I did last time, which was ... ." Being able to laugh at yourself has an added bonus, Justice notes: It helps you tolerate and even accept your own and others' imperfections.

- Make playfulness part of your joint work on projects. The more absurd the play, the better, says Justice. For example, "attacking" each other with squirt guns or nerf balls can help loosen up the group and get ideas flowing.

Justice begins all of his presentations, even those to CEOs, by having participants stand up and introduce themselves to someone they don't know. But here's the twist: "They can't use 'I' or 'I'm,'" explains Justice. "They can only use 'me' when introducing and then giving one or two facts about themselves. So it's 'Me Jeff, me speaker.' Doing something silly like this gets us all laughing at ourselves — and brings us together as a group."

- If "lightening up" is difficult for some people, go back to the basics. A fear of looking foolish, losing control of the situation, or admitting we're not perfect can all be behind our reluctance to laugh. Justice's remedy: "Force yourself out of your comfort zone by taking classes that challenge you. Put yourself in the position of the student, when you have little or no previous knowledge or experience and you're under someone else's guidance."

Putting your ego on the line by becoming a student again, Justice says, will help you regain your joy of learning and get relief from the humorless drive for perfection.

'LIGHTEN UP' ON THE SMALL STUFF

Making mountains out of molehills is often why interpersonal conflict occurs in the workplace, maintains Roslyn Kunin, executive director of the Laurier Institution and president of Roslyn Kunin and Associates in Vancouver, British Columbia.

Kunin says minor irritants such as a boss's gruffness or a colleague's tasteless joke may be magnified all out of proportion to their seriousness. Brushing off isolated incidents of bad temper, poor manners, and lack of judgment goes a long way toward decreasing conflicts.

She also cautions that being seen as humorless can do irreparable harm to your professional reputation. People don't want to work with grumps. Kunin's advice: Lighten up on the small stuff and be more tolerant and forgiving toward those who don't always behave the way you would like them to.

ACTION IDEA

Used at the right time, humor can help you make a serious point. Consider the secretary who took five calls — all unreturned — from the same person for her boss. Finally, the sympathetic secretary wrapped all five messages in a red ribbon and handed them to her boss with a note: "The person is on hold, here are his five messages. It would be a real gift if you'd talk to him." The boss chuckled — and took the call.

BUGGED BY BAD BEHAVIOR?

It's so easy to annoy or offend people without even realizing it. Certain behaviors can drive away customers, alienate coworkers, and cost you your boss's trust and favor. Think of other people's habits that really get to you. Then think again: Do you unconsciously exhibit these behaviors too? To help you acknowledge any annoying habits you might have, ask yourself if you:

- Call people by their first names without being asked.
- Eat or drink while you're talking on the telephone.
- Monopolize the conversation and talk when you should be listening.
- Borrow supplies or equipment without asking.
- Laugh too loudly at inappropriate times.
- Belittle others' concerns or problems.

Eliminate any of those habits you exhibit and you'll make great strides in improving relations with coworkers and customers.

SEVEN SINS AGAINST COWORKERS

Make sure you're not guilty of the "seven deadly sins" of serving those very important internal customers, your coworkers. Here are those "sins," and the way to avoid them, as explained by Dr. Rick Kirschner, an Ashland, Oregon-based speaker, and corporate trainer, in his book *Dealing With People You Can't Stand* (McGraw-Hill).

Sin #1: Coldness — when you get so enmeshed in job details that you come across as uncaring to coworkers.

To avoid this sin: Make an effort to look at and greet coworkers. Say their names during conversation, smile, and, when appropriate, thank them.

Sin #2: The brush-off — when you brush off coworkers who ask for help by saying, in effect, "That's not my job."

To avoid this sin: Show coworkers where they can go for the help they need: "You want to talk to Marion, in Accounting. That's her specialty.'"

Sin #3: Apathy — when you don't know that what you do matters.

To avoid this sin: First, think about how your job is necessary to your company, another department, and to customers. Next, show coworkers that you care about what you and they do.

Sin #4: Condescension — when you have control over what your coworkers want and use your position to condescend to them and act as if you are more powerful.

To avoid this sin: Treat coworkers as an equal part of your team. Think: "We are both working together to find a solution to one of our problems."

ACTION IDEA

One of the best ways to change coworkers' behavior is to lead by your own example. Don't extend your breaks or lunch hour. Leave on time or later at the end of the day, but never before your scheduled departure time.

If your coworkers see you strictly adhering to company rules, they'll feel pressure to follow suit.

Sin #5: Resorting to policy rather than understanding — when you refer to the "rule book" to explain why you can't grant coworkers' requests.

To avoid this sin: First, know why policies are in place. Then, ask your coworker to allow you the opportunity to explain why you have to take a particular position. Says Kirschner: "Asking first makes people more receptive to hearing you."

Sin #6: You act robotic — when you say things like "Have a nice day" in a flat, meaningless way.

To avoid this sin: "Keep in mind that each internal customer is a 'someone' you can serve, not just 'another one' who wants you to do something," says Kirschner.

Sin #7. You're evasive, as when you say things like "Our department does not do that" when they request a service your department does not provide.

To avoid this sin: Strive for an attitude that conveys "What can I do to help you solve your problem? The solution you need may not be part of my job, but I'll help as much as I can."

To make yourself a saintly coworker, eliminate these seven deadly sins and make the solutions part of your everyday work attitude.

APOLOGIES CAN RING TRUE

We all make mistakes when dealing with coworkers. But it's how we make amends that really counts. Accepting responsibility is key to powerful apologies.

How can you apologize well?

- Be sincere. Admit what you did or didn't do.

- State the problem once. Then move on to what you did to resolve it to re-establish goodwill.

- Don't rehash. Stick to how the problem was rectified.

- Explain. For complicated situations, you may need to explain (without being defensive) how the mistake happened and that it was unintentional.

- State your intentions. Make it clear that you intend to maintain a good working relationship and that you hope the other individual will do the same.

- Build safety valves. Outline how you intend to guard against future mistakes.

- Don't overdo it. One apology is sufficient. Get on with today's business.

- Apologize with action. Meet the next deadline, or offer your support in a crisis.

WHEN THE CHILD IN YOU COMES OUT AT WORK

How you react to situations in adulthood often results from childhood experiences, and those experiences can follow you right into the office. These ingrained childhood experiences may manifest themselves in many ways, says psychotherapist Brian DesRoches, author of *Your Boss Is Not Your Mother* (William Morrow and Company).

For example, asks DesRoches, "If your boss unexpectedly asks to see you in his office, what's your first thought? He's going to applaud you for your efforts? Your salary is going to be amended to reflect your hard work?

"Hardly" he says. "You automatically assume you are in trouble. That is a learned reaction from childhood. Oftentimes, when a parent formally asked to speak to you, it was to admonish you, not praise you," he explains. "This is a common reaction that we carry into adulthood."

Your ingrained reactions can impact your rapport with coworkers. If someone at the office rarely acknowledges you, you might assume he or she dislikes you. "Common reactions would be to overcompensate by doing nice things for that person or completely withdraw from the situation," says DesRoches. "These reactions are similar to those we had as children when the other kids rejected us."

What should you do instead? "Confront the individual," he advises. "Explain how you interpret his or her behavior toward you."

Unfortunately, Des Roches adds, people will rarely do this. "Instead, they act on their perceptions, which are incorrect 99 percent of the time. But, the harm is done because those individuals allow those perceptions to color how they feel about themselves."

Reacting to childhood perceptions not only impacts how you deal with people, but it also impacts your work. "What we don't talk about, we act out," explains DesRoches. "For instance, you might subconsciously sabotage your work by becoming distracted because the situation has you emotionally charged. Or, you might introduce a third party into the situation by talking to someone about the other individual." This, says DesRoches, inevitably impacts productivity.

In fact, statistics show that approximately 40 percent to 60 percent of work time is spent resolving emotional conflicts with coworkers. DesRoches calls this "emotional noise." How do you turn down the volume on emotional noise? DesRoches recommends that you analyze your reactions and try to find nonpersonal reasons for workplace occurrences. "You'll end up feeling better about yourself and your work environment."

TROUBLE AHEAD: A COWORKER ABUSES OFFICE PRIVILEGES

Suppose you see a coworker using the telephone for unlimited personal calls, or taking part in some other questionable behavior. How should you handle the situation? Emily Post's *Emily Post on Business Etiquette* (Harper & Row) specifically discusses these and other abuses of office privileges. Post offers the following suggestions:

- Find out the rules. For example, some companies allow employees a minimum number of personal calls and permit use of the photocopier or other equipment. If that's the case, your coworker may not actually be violating a policy. On the other hand, some have more stringent rules and frown upon such uses.

- Remember your company's bottom line. Company expenses and company time are important issues. Your goals should contribute to your company's success, not detract from it.

- Be professional. Follow business etiquette guidelines. Set an example for the coworker in question and others who fall into the same category. Don't cover for coworkers who need work done while they attend to unapproved personal business. Helping them out makes you a contributor to their unethical behavior.

10 TIPS FOR GETTING ALONG BETTER

Are you often frustrated at how difficult it is to get along with others? You can make it easier by following these 10 basic rules established many years ago by Norman Vincent Peale.

1. Remember people's names.
2. Be a comfortable (not stressful) person to be with.
3. Lighten up. Do not let every little thing get you down.
4. Give humility a chance. Don't be a know-it-all.
5. Be an interesting person to know. Work to cultivate a variety of interests so that others will find your company intellectually stimulating.
6. Stop behaviors that obviously annoy other people.
7. Offer your support to those who need it.
8. Make an effort to like people. Eventually, it'll come naturally.
9. Try to clear up misunderstandings and deal with grievances that drain your energy.
10. Clarify your values and beliefs, and develop spiritual depth. Use your inner strength to help others.

ACTION IDEA

In a large office, it can be difficult getting to know everyone. Try this: Organize a monthly get together, where everyone can meet and get to know each other. It's a nice break from the normal routine and provides a set time to socialize. An added advantage: When your coworkers know a time is scheduled for socializing, they may cut down on the socializing that goes on the rest of the month.

ARE YOU FLEXING ENOUGH?

Flexing your personal style to accommodate others is key to more productive relationships, say Robert Bolton and Dorothy Grover Bolton, co-authors of *People Styles at Work: Making Bad Relationships Good and Good Relationships Better* (AMACOM). The Boltons have these suggestions for fast-paced "Expressives," who tend to overwhelm the easygoing "Amiables":

- Talk slower. Don't put yourself at a disadvantage by talking too fast for the amiable person. He or she won't be able to keep up well enough to understand your point.

- Allow adequate time on deadlines. Amiables aren't well suited for rushing to get things done.

- Don't expect quick decision making. "There are times when these slow deciders [amiables] need a nudge," the Boltons note. "But unless time is of the essence, let them make decisions on their own schedule."

- Listen more, talk less. You'll have better luck establishing rapport with quiet amiables.

The key point: Match the communication needs of the other person and you'll have greater success with coworkers.

3 PROVEN STRATEGIES FOR GAINING COOPERATION

Knowing how to get people's attention — and their cooperation — is one of the most useful job skills. It can make all the difference in your ability to get things done, whether you're "pitching" a hot new idea to improve a routine procedure or trying to bring a key project in on time.

Linda Adams of Burlington, Ontario, a trainer with the American Management Association, recommends three proven strategies for getting people to help you get things done:

1. Actively "sell" the ideas you believe in.

a. Use the language of selling, which emphasizes benefits. You can call attention to the benefits of your ideas with phrases such as: "This procedure is easy to implement," "I can guarantee that this will work for us," "This program has been proven to reduce errors by...," "We can save money / time by," and "We can improve our performance ratings by ... ."

b. Avoid the words *should* and *shouldn't*. "Most of us tend to rebel when told what to do," notes Adams.

c. Don't express yourself in a way that implies doubt or hesitancy, such as, "I think this will work." Use phrases of conviction, such as, "I recommend," "I'm convinced," or "I'm confident that ... ."

2. **Get past the defenses of reluctant participants.** Doubt in their ability to meet the group's expectations is often at the root of people's lack of cooperative spirit, Adams points out. She recommends diplomatic guidance to help them get involved. Try these steps:

a. Express faith in the individual's abilities. Let the person know that you are confident in his or her ability to handle a given project.

b. Ask for input. Help the person maintain a clear focus on the ultimate goal. "Your objective is to encourage a reluctant coworker in the direction the rest of the group wants to go, so you need to emphasize the need to aim for common goals," Adams explains. "Don't discourage your coworker with negative responses such as, 'Your idea won't work.'"

c. Make a joint commitment to action. "Once you've discussed and agreed upon a course of action," notes Adams, "ask the other person to verbalize his or her understanding of the commitment."

d. Be diplomatic if you need to clarify the course of action. "Again, don't be negative, as in 'No, that's not how we agreed to do it,'" says Adams. "Instead, use the 'what' approach. Tell your coworker, 'I'm not exactly sure what our agenda is here; can you explain what you mean?'"

3. **Involve everyone in troubleshooting.** For example, if it looks like your work group is not going to meet an important deadline, hold an emergency planning session or redesign the game plan. Seeking everyone's involvement in the solution makes them feel part of the solution. As a result, they'll be more interested in cooperating.

HOW TO EARN TRUST

"The trust of our coworkers is not automatic. It must be earned with behavior that reflects integrity, consideration, and caring," says Susan B. Wilson, owner of the Newton, Iowa-based Executive Strategies and author of *Your Intelligent Heart* (AMACOM).

For example, be willing to admit your mistakes. "Think how uncomfortable you feel around people who try to come across as perfect," Wilson says. "That discomfort comes from the fact that you know no one is perfect. We tend to be drawn to — and more trusting of — people who acknowledge their mistakes."

When you know you've blown it, or you've hurt someone, have the courage to own up and say you're sorry. Admitting your mistakes is a great way to make something positive out what could have become a very negative situation, Wilson observes. "People will recognize your courage in making yourself vulnerable and taking responsibility for your actions. They'll know that you're showing respect when you admit you've stepped on their toes." Here are more suggestions on building trust:

- Share information. "Knowledge may be power, but withholding information doesn't make you look powerful," Wilson maintains. "It diminishes you, conveying the impression that you're insecure and weak. Sharing information, on the other hand, leads to trust, and it invites sharing on the part of others. Information sharing helps us all do our jobs, especially when it comes to solving problems, planning, making decisions, and setting priorities."

- Working for the good of the whole, not just for your own good. "The people we work with know when our primary concern is, 'What's in it for me?'" Wilson emphasizes. "We earn respect and loyalty when we can put aside our own egos and support what's best for the team or the organization."

- When you seek input from others, specify what type and how it will be used. People get confused and resentful when their opinions or ideas are solicited and then ignored, Wilson points out. They also want to know whether they're part of the decision-making process, or simply responding to decisions already made.

- Act ethically. "Even though a certain action may be legal," Wilson says, "it's not necessarily ethical. Whenever you're in doubt about the ethics of some action you're considering, ask yourself, 'If I do this, will I feel comfortable looking at myself in the mirror in the morning?'"

MAKE OFFICE POLITICS WORK FOR YOU

Office politics. When most employees hear those words, they think of "old boy" networks, bureaucracy, and decisions made for reasons not necessarily in the best interest of everyone concerned.

But hold it!

Office politics aren't all bad, says Andrew Denka, executive director of OfficeTeam, an administrative support staffing firm. "Office politics are basic to the business world," says Denka. "If allowed to get out of hand, they can be destructive, but, dealt with properly, office politics enable work to be accomplished smoothly."

Wise workers are conscious of how office politics work. They also learn to use them to their advantage. "Employees who want to advance their careers must learn to make use of the positive diplomacy aspects of office politics while avoiding the negative side," he says.

How can you make office politics work for you? Denka offers these tips:

- Avoid the rumor mill. "If you get caught up in gossip and rumor mongering, you will ultimately damage your professional reputation," says Denka. "You could harm your career or even the future of your company. Never reveal confidential information, and avoid confirming or denying any rumors."

- Build alliances. "Seek to cultivate good relationships with others in your company — it will make your work easier as well as more enjoyable," he says. "Be pleasant and offer help to a committee or join a sports team to form bonds with colleagues outside your department."

- Work on your personal PR. "Your appearance and demeanor reveal a great deal about you," says Denka. "Ability is paramount, but other factors count. To gain respect and be seen as a prime candidate for a promotion, look and act professionally in all circumstances."

- Understand the who, what, and why. "Gain insight into the work style and habits of the people with whom you interact," he suggests. "Does your supervisor prefer written or oral communication? Is your coworker usually less alert early in the morning?

  "Be observant and use what you learn about your colleagues to maximize relationships," Denka advises.

- Cultivate social savvy. "Social situations with coworkers, whether at lunch, after work, or on weekends, can be tricky," he admits. "Be much more careful than you might be with other friends. Whatever you say or do may be back in the office before long."

- Learn to cope with Attila the Hun. "If a coworker loses his or her temper, keep your cool and don't allow yourself to become hostile," says Denka. "Try to leave the scene professionally and diplomatically. Uncontrolled behavior is harmful, no matter how much the other person provoked you."

Remember, it's how you respond to office politics that determines whether they will ultimately help or hurt you in the workplace.

QUICK TIPS

- **Ante up the compliments.** Put 10 pennies in one pocket. Each time you compliment a coworker for a job well done, transfer one penny to the other pocket. Don't let a week go by without emptying your pocket.

- **Say your name.** Here's a tip to help people remember *your* name, from Bill Byrne, author of *Habits of Wealth* (Berkley). Say the other person's name *first,* then yours: "It's nice to meet you, Sharon. My name is Bill Byrne." This technique gives the other person time to listen for your name.

- **Avoid birthday surprises.** Ever been caught unaware of a coworker's birthday? To avoid this, keep a handful of general birthday cards and two small presents in your desk drawer. When the news breaks, you'll be ready to express your best wishes.

- **Morning coffee and e-mail.** Start each day by reviewing your e-mail. Not responding promptly to messages makes you appear unprofessional, nonresponsive, and rude. Checking the mail first thing in the morning helps assure the job gets done before you get busy with other matters.

- **Set the tone.** The next time a coworker asks the obligatory, "How are you?" respond with a hearty "Great!" Your enthusiasm will help set a positive tone.

- **Two good reasons to seek advice.** If you have trouble getting along with one of your teammates, ask for his or her advice on a problem you're experiencing. People like to know their opinion is valued. You just may be able to break down old barriers — and gain some good advice in the process.

QUIZ

'Am I Just Too Concerned About Getting Along?'

"Is it possible to be too concerned about getting along with others? I sometimes give in on important decisions to win coworkers' approval —even when I know I'm right. Later, I'm depressed because I've agreed to something I didn't feel good about."

R. T. K., Lawrence, Kansas

Getting along with others is essential to a successful and harmonious workplace. But don't compromise your ideals just so others will like you. Doing so could be a sign of low self-esteem. The following quiz can help you gauge your esteem level. Score 2 points if you agree (A) with the statement, 1 if you have neutral (N) feelings, and 0 if you disagree (D).

1. If a coworker dislikes me, I generally feel like a less worthwhile human being. _____

2. When someone criticizes me, I have good reason to be upset. _____

3. I usually give up my own interests to please others. _____

4. My value as a person depends greatly on what others think of me. _____

5. I feel I should be upset with myself if I make a mistake. _____

6. My reason for doing a good job is to get other people to like me. _____

7. If my ideas are rejected, I blame my approach rather than the ideas. _____

8. When I start a new project, I imagine everything that could go wrong. _____

9. If someone asks me to do something, I usually feel it is necessary to do it. _____

10. I generally trust other people's choices and decisions more than my own. _____

Your approval-seeking level: If your score was between 14 and 20, you base your self-image almost entirely on how others see you. Remember, your thoughts and actions have as much value as those of others. A score of seven to 13 suggests you look down on yourself more than you should. A score of six or below shows you have a healthy self-esteem level.

YOUR CAREER SURVIVAL TAKE-AWAY

The 2nd simple thing you *must* do to keep your job today (*and* tomorrow)

Develop winning ways with coworkers

In today's volatile job market, the ability to work well with new groups of people quickly and effectively has become an important benchmark of employability. Potential employers don't just evaluate job applicants on their skills. They want to know how well the employee will work with others. Managers don't just appraise you on the amount of time you spend at your desk; they want to know that you're a team player and that you can rally the support of your coworkers to achieve your mutual goals. Don't take for granted your ability to work well with others. Refine the techniques that improve communication and increase teamwork — it's time well spent that will further your career potential.

WHAT YOU CAN DO

In today's work environment, it simply is not realistic to assume you will work with the same group of people for your entire working life. But don't let that stop you from cultivating friendships with coworkers. Making friends with someone you work with can make your job more enjoyable and will enrich your life. A friendship at work is more likely to succeed if you keep work and friendship issues separate and both agree not to use your relationship to get favors.

- **Don't overlook the value of positive office politics.** Used properly, office politics helps the work get completed more smoothly. At all costs, avoid the negative aspects of office politics, such as backstabbing and tuning in to the rumor mill. Focus instead on the positive aspects of office politics that can help you grow professionally and improve how you are viewed at work.

- **Don't overlook the value of humor.** Used properly, it can ease tensions and build better relationships with coworkers.

- **Brush up the basics.** Using people's names in conversation, complimenting coworkers for a job well done, offering support to those who need it, and making an effort to like people ... these skills require your constant attention. Don't get so caught up in your daily deadlines and other work pressures that you forget to give your attention to the simple techniques that make you someone with whom others enjoy working.

CHAPTER THREE

Simple Thing #3:
MEET AND *EXCEED* YOUR BOSS'S EXPECTATIONS

"When a person thinks he is putting it over on the boss,
the boss is not thinking of putting him over others to boss."

— C.K. ANDERSON

INTRODUCTION

In reality, no one is completely indispensable in today's work environment. But even if you believe that everyone can be replaced, you also have to believe that some people are more dispensable than others. Certainly there are people you work with whose performance (or lack of performance) makes them prime candidates for the first round of pink slips when cutbacks are in order.

In all likelihood, those employees haven't learned a fundamental lesson of workplace survival, that is, *the only way to come close to guaranteeing job security is to make yourself too valuable to lose.* And the best way to do that is to make yourself indispensable to your boss.

Of course, even your boss can't make guarantees about the future. He or she could be on the way out the door during the next wave of layoffs. But your best chance of succeeding and proving your overall value to your organization is by teaming up with your boss to work toward his or her organizational and professional goals.

To be sure you're on the same wavelength as your boss, Patti Hathaway and Susan D. Schubert suggest setting up a meeting with your supervisor to discuss goals. "Let your boss know you're aiming to improve your performance and that you want your goals to be right in synch with the company's," Hathaway and Schubert suggest in *Managing Upward: Strategies for Succeeding with Your Boss* (Crisp Publications, Inc). They also recommend:

- Adding a discussion of common goals to the agenda for an upcoming team meeting.

- Paying close attention to key words and phrases used by management. These reflect the organization's direction and goals. You might find key terms such as "customer service," "innovation," and "excellence" repeated frequently on bulletin boards and in company newsletters, annual reports, and advertising.

- Identifying themes that repeatedly come up in meetings such as taking responsibility for decision making or building customer loyalty.

Meeting and exceeding your boss's expectations doesn't mean you and your boss will always agree or that you should reduce your worth to the position of "yes" man or woman. It means forming a partnership with your boss —making sure you're both on the same wavelength about what he or she wants to accomplish and the role you play in seeing that those goals are met. You can't predict the future, but by meeting and exceeding your boss's expectations, you're drawing a road map that can help point you in the direction you want your future to take.

WHAT WOULD YOU DO?

GAMES WE PLAY WITH THE BOSS

You like and admire your boss. But sparks fly almost every time the two of you interact. You can't agree on anything.

Are you taking the relationship too personally, instead of focusing on the professionalism that can benefit you both? asks Ruth Siress, author of *Working Woman's Communications Survival Guide* (Prentice Hall).

Think about your most recent interactions with your boss. Is your behavior contributing to the tension? Look for:

- **Avoidance.** When a conflict or threat of disagreement arises, do you withdraw and avoid discussing the issue?

- **Passive-aggressive behavior.** Do you criticize your boss for an inability to solve a crisis you yourself won't tackle? Do you engage in subtle sabotage, such as not doing your best, in the hope that it will hurt your boss's reputation?

- **Undermining.** Do you actually look for negatives in your boss and disagree about nearly everything he or she says?

- **Fear.** Are you afraid that your professional image and position will suffer if your boss is successful? Step back to take a close look at your thinking.

"It's a reality in corporate life that making your boss look good makes you look good," Siress emphasizes. It pays to be supportive and to encourage your boss's success as much as you can. That can only enhance your own success.

UNDERSTAND YOUR BOSS'S STYLE

You may have your own classification for the type of boss you work for. According to William J. Morin, chairman of the outplacement firm of Drake Bean Morin Inc., bosses generally fall into four categories. Adjusting to the boss's style is crucial to your success.

- Thinkers. Logical, rational, and structured, thinkers value information and systematic inquiry. When problems arise, they consider each aspect, and weigh all the options before they decide on the best course of action. They rely on observation and judgment, and avoid emotion or speculation.

  Thinkers are easy to spot: Their offices are usually meticulously clean and orderly. Their desks are immaculate, with only what they are currently working on in sight. Clothing is neat with matching accessories. To get your ideas across to a thinker boss, document your presentation with facts, figures, whys, and hows. Your evidence must be beyond reproach. You'll be asked questions, so try to anticipate them and formulate answers beforehand.

- Feelers. Empathetic and emotional, they place a high value on personal interaction. They usually have superior people skills, and encourage employees to stop by any time. Their offices are warm and friendly with a collection of personal objects placed about.

  To pitch an idea to a feeler, make your presentation colorful and appealing. Focus on a more emotional appeal. Use friendly familiar language. Well-placed humor can work wonders.

- Intuitors. These imaginative, creative people place a high value on ideas and theories, and are usually involved in a wide variety of projects. They tend to be spontaneous and "off the wall." Their offices are filled with a wide variety of unusual items, and their desks look like a filing cabinet that exploded. Often there are books piled on, particularly surveys or theoretical works. Most intuitors are more concerned with performance than appearance.

  To present an idea to intuitors, avoid the traditional presentation. Your originality is key to your idea's success. Avoid bogging down the boss with intricate details; he or she is looking for the "big picture." Don't be surprised if your pitch turns into a brainstorming session. Your idea may spark others the boss may have.

- Sensers. Results-oriented, assertive, and pragmatic, sensers value action and like to get things done without needless deliberation. They are constantly in motion, and are usually described as workaholics. Their desks are typically cluttered, as they are too busy to be neat. Most work with their jackets off and sleeves rolled up.

  A no-nonsense, direct approach is what these people look for. Be concrete about the steps you take to make your idea a reality. Be economical with words and facts. Highlight the anticipated net results.

NEW BOSS? GIVE THE RELATIONSHIP SOME TIME

As mergers and downsizings become more common in the workplace, the likelihood that you may one day have to adjust to a new boss has increased. If you've been loyal to the same boss for a long time, it may be even more challenging for you to adapt to a new boss if the change is sudden and unexpected. However, it's important not to underestimate the influence your first few days with a new manager can have on your entire working relationship.

Here are tips for starting off on the right foot with your new boss:

- Give yourself time to adjust. It's natural to feel sad, perhaps even angry, depending on the circumstances of the previous boss's departure. Accept these feelings as a normal part of "letting go," but keep them separate from the relationship you develop with the new boss.

- Clarify expectations. Some managers initiate individual meetings with employees as part of the "getting-to-know-you" process. If your new manager doesn't, you can initiate such a meeting yourself. State that you'd like to learn more about his or her overall style and expectations of you. Some people even present a new boss with their resumés, so the boss can learn about the skills, experience, and expertise of staff members. Or ask your new boss what he or she thinks distinguishes an adequate performer from an exemplary one.

- Avoid negative comments about people in the organization. It may be tempting during those first few days to give your boss the real lowdown on individuals in the company from your perspective. Resist this temptation if you want to retain your credibility as a professional.

- Resist comparisons. Every manager brings a unique set of strengths and weaknesses to the job. Avoid referring constantly to what your previous boss used to do, particularly if it's clear that your new manager has different ideas. If you are asked about past procedure, answer honestly, but avoid making it sound like your previous manager's approach was the only "right" way. Accept that your new boss will do things differently, and remain open-minded about new ideas.

- Provide opportunities to learn about your work. It's likely the boss wants to begin getting involved in department activities, but may be unsure of priorities. Ask his or her opinion on something you are working on, or just provide an update on a big project you may have started under the direction of your former boss.

Above all, give yourself time to adjust to each other's styles. Although we occasionally meet people we automatically "click" with, usually it takes a few months to become comfortable working with a new boss. Meanwhile, it's likely your new manager wants to start off on the right foot as much as you, and would welcome your efforts to make him or her more comfortable.

HEY CHIEF, SLOW DOWN!

Idea people are extremely valuable to a company, but occasionally need help converting their ideas and goals into bottom-line results. Consider, for example, a boss who sets challenging goals for you, but then shifts gears before you can get the job done. As a result, you're unable to meet your deadlines.

"Start by trying to slow down your boss," says management consultants Christopher Hegarty and Philip Goldberg in *How to Manage Your Boss* (Rawson, Wade). Ask her to explain what she is trying to accomplish. Each time she shifts gears, ask her — without challenging her — to clarify her goals. Point out what goals or tasks must be abandoned to adopt the new

ACTION IDEA

If your boss continues at a pace that's three steps ahead of you, you may have to pin down your boss on a particular project with an agreement to let you see it through to completion by a certain date.

strategy. Make her think things through by bringing up facts to support your concerns. "In a noncritical moment, you might say, 'Your ideas are great, but sometimes I have difficulty keeping up with you. How can I work with you so that I can become more valuable to you?'" say the authors.

When your supervisor fires off a new idea, Hegarty and Goldberg suggest waiting a short period of time, in anticipation of another major priority shift, before you begin acting on it.

MIRROR THE WAY YOUR BOSS THINKS

If you believe that in the workplace reward comes to the deserving, think again, says Barry Eigen, in *How To Think Like A Boss And Get Ahead At Work* (Avon Books). When Eigen was a manager and sought to promote an employee, he didn't seek someone who "deserved" it, but rather someone he felt had the necessary traits and capabilities to handle the job — someone who had traits similar to his.

"The ultimate truth," says Eigen, "is that managers don't promote people because of what they are doing today; they promote them for what they believe they can do tomorrow. Often, those people have characteristics that mirror the boss. You need to demonstrate your ability to understand how your work fits into the overall goals of the company and then do what you can to contribute reaching those goals."

Eigen devised a list of what he call the "magnificent seven" qualities that managers seek when choosing candidates for promotion.

1. The courage to take risks, make mistakes, and admit when you don't know something. Doing the expected, remaining within the realm of your job description, is merely riding on the wave of mediocrity. Those who excel in the workplace take the extra step. How well they do doesn't matter as much as the fact that they tried.

2. The ability to think. Those who have the ability to think don't just do their jobs; they think about what their jobs mean to the company and how they fit into the bigger picture.

3. Honesty. Honest people are willing to admit their mistakes or admit that they don't understand something. You can't improve until you admit there is something to improve.

4. The ability to communicate. Usually, the best communication is short and concise. "Sometimes the clearest communicators are those who say the least," says Eigen. "Many people tend to say too much and overexplain themselves. When you say too much, you drown out the actual message that you want to convey."

5. The ability and the initiative. Managers value people who don't have to be told what to do. They look for those who know what to do and then do it.

6. An understanding of what constitutes good service. "These employees know what service to provide to make the next sale," says Eigen. "They don't just quit once a sale is over. They continue to serve that customer and get him or her to keep coming back."

7. The ability to see into the future. You don't have to be a fortune-teller, but you do need the vision to see what lies ahead for your organization. Most companies today know that reengineering meets the needs of the changing marketplace. You need vision to see what those changes are as well.

Most managers have many of these traits, or at least believe they do. Show your manager that you do, too, and you will lay the groundwork for your future.

BOSS BONDING

Never underestimate the importance of getting along with your boss, says Andrew Sherwood, president of Goodrich & Sherwood Co., a human resources consulting firm. To be an effective employee, Sherwood offers the following tips:

- Understand your boss and the context in which he or she works, including goals, pressures of the position, strengths, weaknesses, blind spots, and preferred work style.

- Assess your abilities and needs, including strengths, weaknesses, and predisposition toward authority figures.

- Develop and maintain a relationship suitable to your needs and work style, and to those of your boss.

LISTEN YOUR WAY TO JOB SUCCESS

Contrary to popular belief, you can't talk your way to success, but you can listen your way there, says Roger Ailes, author of *You Are The Message* (Doubleday). You should spend 60 percent to 70 percent of your day listening to others and the remainder talking, suggests Ailes. Listening helps you concentrate better on what others are saying. At work, listening increases your chances of understanding your boss's instructions and getting them right on the first try.

Do it often enough, and you're bound to see positive results.

ACTION IDEA

In Business Briefs (Peterson's), by Russ Wild, business psychologist Michael W. Mercer suggests mirroring your boss's physical actions. "If the boss leans toward you, lean toward him. If he speaks quickly, speak quickly. If he speaks slowly, speak slowly," says Mercer. "People crave to be around similar people."

PERFORMANCE BOOSTS

Want management to sit up and take notice of your performance? Barry Eigen, in *How to Think Like a Boss and Get Ahead at Work* (Carol Publishing Group), suggests keeping these six guiding principles in mind:

1. Fix it before it leaks. Look for workable solutions to problems and then take them to the boss. Avoid petty gripes.

2. Remember that nobody's perfect. Not even you. Admit mistakes, shortcomings, and imperfections rather than trying to deny them or cover them up. Employees who "never make mistakes" suggest that they are playing it so safe that they lack creativity and confidence.

3. Avoid the entitlement trap. Raises and promotions are earned by performing beyond expectations. They are not automatically guaranteed.

4. Sell yourself. Find opportunities to outline your skills and accomplishments. Express your willingness to take on more responsibility. Bosses are usually so busy that they may not notice every individual's strengths until someone else brings them to their attention.

5. Give yourself a chance. Trust yourself to grow into new assignments, even though you might worry at first about the extra load. Don't wait for the perfect moment to seize an opportunity. It will never come.

6. Make the right friends. Cultivate friendships with upbeat peers. And don't forget to strike up alliances with those on higher levels. Avoid the complainers, naysayers, and nitpickers.

WANT TO SUCCEED? VOLUNTEER FOR MORE WORK

Looking for an effective way to get that coveted raise or hard-to-get promotion? Who isn't? What's the answer? Ask for more work, advise 82 percent of top managers in a new nationwide survey.

The survey, developed by OfficeTeam, polled 150 human resource and other executives from the nation's 1,000 largest companies.

It's no secret that personal initiative is a valuable asset for career development — management looks for "go-getters" among its ranks when filling available positions. This was confirmed when surveyed executives were asked: "What do you feel is the single best way for employees to earn a promotion or a raise?" Their responses shouldn't be too surprising. The vast majority (82 percent) answered, "Ask for more work and responsibility." Eleven percent answered, "Publicize achievements." However, a greater workload may not mean more time on the job.

ACTION IDEA

Think of one new responsibility you can ask your boss about taking on. Be specific. Be sure you know:

• How the responsibility will benefit the organization

• How you will grow professionally taking on the new task

• How you will accomplish the job without overloading yourself or compromising the work you do now

Only 2 percent answered, "Work longer hours," as a means to advance a career. That should come as some relief to those who have responsibilities outside the workplace environment. The remaining 5 percent provided some other answer.

"By asking for more responsibility and an increased workload, employees demonstrate that they're self-motivated and enthusiastic about their jobs," says Andrew Denka, executive director of OfficeTeam. "Managers recognize and reward employees who display that kind of initiative and personal investment in their companies," he states.

Certainly, this doesn't mean that you should assume so much work that you come to the end of your tether and end up stressed out and ineffective. That would certainly work against your career goals. However, one way to show initiative, Denka says, is to take an extra step when doing a task, as in the case of an administrative assistant who volunteers to set up a new, computerized database when asked to reorganize existing files.

Going above and beyond the call of duty provides an opportunity to display skills that may otherwise go unnoticed. It also can set you apart from less-motivated colleagues. Denka adds that requests for more work suggest that an employee can manage his or her schedule efficiently, achieving more in the same amount of time. This becomes critical as companies condense their workforces to streamline operations and boost bottom-line profitability. We're not suggesting that you kill yourself trying to get ahead. Rather, you might be smart to selectively do more than the job actually requires. The result might amaze you — and your boss!

CARRY OUT INSTRUCTIONS WITH FLAIR

In a perfect workplace, we would all know what to do, and there would really be no need to listen to or follow instructions. But in the real world, following instructions is an integral part of the work experience, applicable to everything from running photocopy machines to handling special assignments from the boss.

Following instructions is essential to how we relate to those around us and how well we perform at work, says Richard Saul Wurman, author of *Follow the Yellow Brick Road* (Bantam). In every work situation, Wurman notes, there are instruction-givers and instruction-takers. It's the responsibility of the givers to make sure their instructions are clear and detailed, although often this is not the case. Responsibility for carrying out the task and getting the job done falls to the instruction takers. Following instructions is not instinct. Nor should it be a robotic routine. It is a skill. Here are Wurman's suggestions to improve your performance as an instruction-taker:

- Interpret and respond. After receiving instructions, repeat them to the giver in your own words, either verbally or in a memo. This way, both parties will agree on what's to be done before any action is initiated. If you have a suggestion or wish to offer a modification of the instructions, feel free to do so. If you don't think you're the appropriate person to carry out the instruction, say so.

- Clear up confusion. If you don't understand something, ask for clarification. It's better to suffer some embarrassment up front than to discover later that you've wasted time and energy in doing the wrong thing.

- Be alert for faulty instructions. Many instructions aren't followed properly because they aren't presented correctly. Check for these defects: abstract terms that lack mutual interpretation, messages with so much detail that the essence is lost, missing steps, and no deadlines.

- Choose your response. Taking instruction requires choices. You can ignore it, deliberately botch it, do the minimum, or consider it as a learning experience and a way to enhance your work performance. The first three options are obviously not recommended. But the important thing to realize is that you must consciously choose your method of responding to an instruction.

- Do a quick check up. Before starting, ask yourself: Do I understand? What am I supposed to accomplish? What is the most direct approach to reach the goal? What are alternative paths? What are my own interests and aptitudes?

- Report your progress. Even though it may not be requested, update the instruction-giver on your progress at regular intervals. If you need more information, say so. If you need help, alert the boss.

Above all, remember that you are not a machine. You are an active participant in fulfilling instructors' goals.

9 Career Killers

At work, being a poor performer is at least as difficult as being a successful one. After all, you don't just become a failure overnight — it takes hard work and practice. You must constantly strive to be the worst that you can be.

Follow these simple rules to turn off your boss and never get ahead in your career:

1. Never take risks. What could possibly be gained if you rock the boat? People who take risks put everything on the line as they strive to reach new heights — and they are never satisfied. Why bother? If you go that extra mile with a client or coworker, you increase your chances for error.

2. Don't let emotions show. Particularly your enthusiasm. Don't let your work get to you. It's just a job. It's not supposed to be fun. Don't get personally involved with people or projects at any cost. Showing concern for your work or your coworkers must be avoided at all costs!

3. Always have an excuse ready. This takes practice. At first, you may find yourself being humble or responsible, but with practice, you can avoid taking the blame for anything. Start with: "The customer doesn't know what he's talking about"; "I'd do better if I got some help"; and the old stand-by, "How was I supposed to know?" Don't make your excuses too creative. That imaginative urge may spill into your job performance.

4. Point out faults in others. Image is everything. Only by criticizing coworkers can you maintain your status. Get them before they get you. Study others and how they perform, analyze their flaws, and criticize them in front of peers and bosses. And be as scathing and biting as possible when you do.

5. Forget about customer courtesy. Customers interfere with your work. So why be polite to them? Get real! "Good afternoon," "please," and "thank you" are extraneous comments that nobody listens to anyway. If someone tells you, "have a nice day," demand that they tell you how.

6. Beware of uniqueness. Eliminate any traits that make you stick out from the crowd. Aim for the mediocre. Otherwise, others will expect too much from you.

7. When problems arise, know whom to blame. Don't burden yourself and take responsibility for what happens on the job. This can only lead to questions and more involvement in sticky issues. The simplest approach is to blame someone else. It helps to have a particular person in mind, a scapegoat who is easy to point the finger at.

8. Avoid professional development. Let's face it. You've gotten where you are on your own merit. Why strive to learn more? Beware of reading materials and skills workshops that try to make you more effective. If you must get involved with any new programs, teach yourself — when you're good and ready. Discourage others from taking part in these programs, or you'll wind up with a bunch of problem solvers who will point the finger at you!

9. Look out for number one. Always put yourself first. Before you take on any new project or any community work — especially if it only pays "goodwill" — always ask, "What's in it for me?" If you will be expected to do more than you do now, demand compensation. Remember that brownie points are inedible and don't pay the rent.

Certainly, there are more ways to achieve the level of inadequacy you desire, but we guarantee that if you follow these simple rules, you'll be a complete failure sooner than you thought possible. You can wave good-bye to any responsibility, promotion, and maybe even your job!

ACTION IDEA

Time for a little honest soul searching. Do any of the career killers strike uncomfortably close to home?

— OK. I ADMIT. I'M GUILTY OF CAREER KILLER # _____ .

— IT IS MOST EVIDENT IN THE WAY I _____

_____

_____

_____

_____

— BUT I WANT TO CHANGE! HERE'S WHAT I'LL DO DIFFERENTLY, STARTING TODAY: _____

_____

_____

_____

_____

COME ON, YOU CAN DO IT: 'FESS UP TO PERFORMANCE ERRORS

Even the most efficient, diligent, and organized employees miss deadlines, make mistakes, or fall behind from time to time. Yes, it can even happen to you. When it does, one of the hardest things to do is to tell the boss about it. Why? You might feel foolish at the mistake, and, worse yet, you may think that your credibility is on the line. The worst thing you can do is to try to cover your tracks, say nothing, and hope nobody finds out. But, people do in time.

Here are some suggestions on how to fill your boss in, while keeping your professional image intact:

- Don't wait. Let the boss know as soon as possible. If you hesitate, you may do further damage to the project and to the boss's trust in you. Then, you will really look incompetent. If your boss knows about the situation, he or she can work around other projects. Whatever you do, don't let the boss find out from another source.

- State your reasons. Your candor will help the boss evaluate the situation accurately. Don't give lame excuses or blame coworkers. If you're in the wrong, admit it and offer a simple apology. There's no need to belabor the error with multiple apologies.

- Present Plans B, C, and D. Few bosses want to know only about the problems. They're interested in solutions, too. If you can present options, you send the message that you've still got a grip on the situation. Present several alternatives. If the boss recommends another plan, accept it. If there's still a conflict, give feedback. Above all, make sure that you fully understand what the boss expects from you to solve the problem. Ask questions. Guessing could worsen the problem.

- Inform others. When the game plan has been changed, spread the word to coworkers who will be affected by the change. You're smart to do this in writing so everyone has a record. Offer your help whenever possible to make the shift easy on your colleagues. Update the boss periodically to reestablish that you're responsible, trustworthy, and on the ball.

- Make notes. Determine what happened and why. At what point did things start to fall apart? Keep these notes on file. Refer to them to prevent a recurrence in the future. It's easy for a boss to forgive a mistake the first time — it's the second time that tests his or her patience and threatens your credibility.

- Let the matter go. Once the project is back on track, don't dwell on your mistake. That will only hinder you in the future.

Missing deadlines, falling behind, and making mistakes aren't tragic in and of themselves. Even your bosses have made their fair share. It's how you react that counts. Your quick, honest response ultimately determines the success of your recovery.

REVIEWS HELP REFINE CAREER GOALS

Some people would rather face a firing squad than sit through a performance review. Others see no difference between the two. A performance review makes them feel demoralized, insulted, embarrassed, and sometimes a little angry. What they don't understand is this: A performance review — even a less-than-stellar one — can be a valuable tool for career development.

Bosses do performance reviews to praise (and sometimes reward) good qualities. They are also meant to point out trouble areas that need improvement. Most importantly, the review focuses on your specific work behaviors, not on you personally.

If your last performance review contained nothing but glorious praise, terrific! Keep improving on what you already do well. It's up to you to discover the subtle improvements that will boost your performance. If your last review was somewhat critical, count yourself lucky in a way. Now you've got a clear direction regarding what you need for a great review next time. Don't wait until two weeks before the next evaluation to whip yourself into shape. Get ahead of the game by starting now.

Take an objective look at yourself. Construct a list of things you do well. Don't be humble here. What do you do better than most? What are your strengths? How do they contribute to the company you work for? Now construct another list. Write down the boss's suggestions for improvement. Add your own personal observations. Where would you like to improve? Be objective here, too.

Compare the two lists. Try to link those things you do well with the areas for improvement. In short, how can your strengths help eliminate your weaknesses? Don't try to tackle every improvement at once because you'll set yourself up for higher stress levels, frustration, and failure.

While you're tackling your areas for improvement, here are some other things to do to increase the chance of getting a better review:

- Come into the office 15 minutes earlier. The boss will be impressed that you're willing to get a jump-start on your day.

- Show potential for other positions in the company. Learn about other departments — how they operate and what tasks their people perform.

- Help your colleagues, if you can. Bosses notice those who contribute to teamwork.

- Be efficient. Complete tasks correctly the first time — aim for zero mistakes. Then, you don't have to backtrack to correct errors.

ACTION IDEA

Be your own best p.r. person. Throughout the year, keep a journal of your personal successes. One item might be something like: "Jan. 15 — Solved Acme's computer problem three hours after their call. Company president complimented me on my speed." Take a few of your journal entries into your performance review. Don't spend the whole time patting yourself on the back. But refer to your notes to support your strengths ("I make a point of responding promptly to customer calls. For example, early in the year, Acme's president personally thanked me for . . . "). The journal is important because you won't remember incidents nine and 10 months down the line.

Don't think of a performance appraisal as a chance for the boss to criticize you. Think of it as a learning experience. Use these evaluations to get ahead in your career. Who knows? The next review might bring you closer to your career goals. So shoot for the stars.

HOW TO FIX A POOR PERFORMANCE DURING YOUR NEXT REVIEW

How do you make the best of a poor performance review? Make arrangements to meet with your evaluator as soon as possible to discuss your recent evaluation. Ask your boss to go over with you again the key points of your recent review. Be sure you understand exactly what it is about your performance that she felt needed improvement. This is not a time to be bashful about asking questions. If you don't understand the explanation of any part of her evaluation, ask that she explain again. You can't improve if you don't know where you are going wrong.

Be clear as well on what steps you are expected to take toward improvement. Sometimes, it's useful to actually spell out these steps in writing so that you both have a "road map" to follow. It may even be specified in a written agreement signed by you and your boss. But be forewarned that honoring the terms of this agreement is crucial to your future success with the company. If you don't keep your end of the deal, you could face disciplinary action or even termination.

Lastly, tell the boss that you'd appreciate suggestions on how you can prepare for your next review. Know your shortcomings, be honest about them, and have solutions in mind. Your reviewer may tell you, for example, "I've noticed that you're almost always several days late submitting your month-end reports." You should already know that and acknowledge it: "Yes, I realize I haven't been completing those reports on time." Then explain how you plan to improve: "In fact, I've already made it one of my goals to have the reports ready for distribution at least three days before the end of each month. And here's how I plan to go about getting that done."

Prove yourself by making sure you meet that goal.

"IF ONLY MY BOSS WOULD . . ."

People complain about their bosses: "If only she would leave me alone." "If only he would help me more." Although no one can change another person's personality, you can adjust *your approach* to improve your relationship:

- Modify behavior. If your boss constantly looks over your shoulder, bring work to her as you complete sections. You may get control over its review — and more breathing room.

- Show initiative. You may feel you need more help from your boss, while he wants to leave details up to you. Keep in mind that he's not a mind reader. Outline a plan of how you should proceed. Then, ask for his comments.

- Demonstrate other abilities. Show that you can handle more than routine assignments. Stress that this will free your boss to do more important tasks.

COMPLAIN WITH PURPOSE

The best complainers are those who offer answers. When something at work doesn't seem to go right, don't just complain about it to your supervisor — offer a suggestion on how to fix it. Often, complaints fall on deaf ears unless they pertain to something that is an obvious workplace priority. Chances are, if you offer a solution, your supervisor will be more inclined to react than if you just presented problems. If you have several complaints, focus on resolving one at a time.

DISAGREE AGREEABLY

Some people can just rub a person the wrong way. They may have good ideas, but the way they present them may cause you to respond emotionally rather than sensibly. The result: an argument.

When that person is your boss, it's even more important to know how to keep control of your emotions so that your attitude doesn't cause problems for you. When a boss says something that gets you riled, you need to learn how to turn a potential argument into a constructive discussion. You also need to learn how to be less confrontational in getting your point across.

Before you start to disagree with your boss, consider what he has to say, suggests Cathy McCrea, a management consultant in Ogden, Utah. "Arguing with your boss will only hurt you in the long run. After all, he is your boss and it is his job to make decisions whether you and your coworkers agree with them or not." Consider what is being said from both perspectives, she advises. "If you still can't see his perspective, there are ways to approach him without becoming confrontational."

McCrea recommends that you wait until you are calm. Then, use the following tips to help you disagree agreeably, and turn a potential argument into a discussion:

1. Listen carefully. Don't think of what you are going to say next as your boss is speaking. You might interpret him incorrectly and steer the conversation off course.

2. Show respect. When you treat another person with consideration and appreciation, you are more likely to have the other person see your point of view.

3. Be positive. Don't immediately reject your boss's viewpoint. "Remember," says McCrea, "it's only a point of view, not a law. Rejecting someone's ideas right away will almost always provoke an argument and cause the other person to be on the defensive throughout the conversation. It is important to remember to always validate the other person's opinion by giving him credit for what he has to say."

4. Use questions. Questions will help you find out what you and your boss agree on. Once you discover your common points, you will be able to proceed with ease in the conversation. This approach also will enable your boss to listen — and maybe even agree — with what you have to say.

5. Have all the facts. Don't base your comments on rumors and assumptions: always have valid facts to back up what you say. Knowing the facts will give you more credibility and respect. Your boss will start seeing your side of things.

QUICK TIPS

- **Take the bullet.** Has the boss ever pointed the finger at you to *his* boss for a mistake he's made? "An insecure boss can't admit he's imperfect," says Alan Weiss, president of Rhode Island-based Summit Consulting Group. His advice: Accept the blame. "Calmly acknowledge the problem, being certain to drop the word 'we' a few times, as in 'Yes, we missed the boat.' This sends the subconscious signal that the department, not just you, screwed up."

- **Stay or leave?** When you're in the boss's office and the telephone rings, should you wait or leave? Etiquette expert Letitia Baldrige says that if your boss motions you to stay, study your notes, look at a magazine, or glance out the window. *Don't* stare or appear to be listening. If the phone call turns personal, she says in her *Complete Guide To Executive Manners* (Rawson Associates), "Get up and quietly go into the waiting area, making a signal that you'll wait there."

- **Bosses have bad days.** With cutbacks and downsizing running rampant, it is easy to look for clues of trouble in everything around us. But if your boss looks sullen or pained, keep your paranoia in check. One secretary looks back now with amusement on the day she thought her boss was going to fire her. "At 4 o'clock when he left early, I discovered he had a toothache all day," she says. "I learned not to read so much into everything!"

- **Say "Yes" to criticism.** If your boss or supervisor complains about you, respond positively. Thank him or her for bringing the problem to your attention. After all, knowing when others aren't satisfied is vital to becoming a top-notch performer.

- **Take more responsibility.** Keep a running log of questions and problems you discuss with your supervisor. Then review it. Ask yourself which problems and questions you could have dealt with yourself. Then begin asking yourself that question *before* you approach your boss with a question.

- **Redirect the review.** During your annual review, your boss focuses only on the negative. Try refocusing the conversation with something like, "I think there's a larger context here. Perhaps we can talk about some of the things that went right this year."

QUIZ

Measuring Up for Your Boss

"I've been on the job for two years, and I've asked my boss several times to give me more to do. He agrees, but so far it hasn't happened. I'm getting really bored. How can I convince my boss to give me more responsibility?"

— *T.L., Missoula, Montana*

You're eager to grow professionally. But you need to prove to your boss that you're ready. Take this quiz to see what you're doing right to earn your boss's trust. Respond YES or NO to each statement and score yourself below.

	YES	NO
1. You enthusiastically carry out all of your responsibilities.	___	___
2. When you complete assignments, you find something else to do instead of socializing or complaining.	___	___
3. You're quick to volunteer when help is needed on emergency tasks.	___	___
4. You present your boss with solutions rather than problems.	___	___
5. You're an idea person who is always proposing ways to do things better, faster, and more efficiently.	___	___
6. You look for ways to help your boss do his or her job more effectively.	___	___
7. You fully understand the mission and goals of your organization and work group.	___	___
8. You take advantage of every opportunity to maintain and upgrade the skills you need to do your job.	___	___
9. You keep up-to-date with changes in your business and industry.	___	___
10. When you ask your boss to entrust you with more work, you offer specific ideas as to what those responsibilities could be.	___	___

TOTAL NUMBER OF YES ANSWERS: _____

How do you measure up? If you responded YES to eight or more of the above statements, you should be well on your way to earning your boss's acceptance of your abilities and potential. If you responded YES to fewer than eight statements, consider how you can boost your performance to a higher level and encourage your boss to support your professional development.

YOUR CAREER SURVIVAL TAKE-AWAY

The 3rd simple thing you must do to keep your job today (and tomorrow)

Meet and exceed *your boss's expectations*

There are no guarantees, but if you want to maximize your job security, you have to position yourself as someone the company wants to keep through good times and bad. One of the best ways to do this is to make your boss happy.

Get to know what your boss expects of you. Meet those expectations and exceed them. Then position yourself as a stand-out performer by helping your boss achieve *her* organizational goals. Create a place for yourself as a valuable partner to your boss. In reality, your value at work really depends on only one factor: how successful you are at making your boss happy. You help yourself professionally each time you act on that simple truth. All your goals and job activities should point toward that one basic goal.

WHAT YOU CAN DO

- **Show that you are someone your boss can depend on.** Volunteer for more work, particularly those thankless jobs that need to be done.

- **Get to know your boss's personality.** What motivates her? What particular quirks are part of her leadership style? The better understanding you have of your boss's personality, the better you can adjust your style to help you get along and work side-by-side with her.

- **Your boss is human.** He needs a pat on the back now and then, too. When you have something positive to say about your boss, share it with him.

- **Don't run to your boss with every crisis and problem that develops.** Get answers, find solutions. Shield your boss from the mundane problems that keep her from focusing on the big picture.

- **Get the most mileage from your performance reviews.** Take a proactive role in your next review. Don't expect your boss to have the full picture of your year's activities. Be prepared to cite your achievements. If any negative points are discussed, learn from them. Discuss specifically what you will do to improve your performance in the year ahead. Stick with that plan.

CHAPTER FOUR

Simple Thing #4:
DEVELOP YOUR POWERFUL COMMUNICATION SKILLS

*"The greatest problem in communication is the illusion that
it has been accomplished."*

— GEORGE BERNARD SHAW (1856–1950), DRAMATIST

INTRODUCTION

The technological revolution has brought us a wealth of new communication tools, including e-mail, satellite communications, video-conferencing, and fax transmissions.

What technology hasn't done is help us communicate better. Consider these three true examples of modern-day office communications:

- Kirk Johansen has worked for a Fortune 100 company for six months. At least once or twice each week he receives some kind of inter-office correspondence. In all this time, he says, "The company has never gotten my name right." His benefits package was addressed to "Kurt Johansen." His first payroll stub was made out to "Kirk Johnson." On one occasion, a memo from human resources was earmarked for "Kurt Jackson." "It really makes you feel pretty unimportant when the company you work for can't get your name right."

- Patricia Marks was looking forward to working with her new supervisor in the loan department of a major bank. She had heard a lot of positive things about the new boss. But on the first day of work, the new supervisor sent a "hello" e-mail to the staff. "It contained so many typos and incomplete sentences, I was shocked," says Patricia. "We all had a good laugh about it ... I mean, this is supposed to be our boss and she can't write a coherent sentence? My respect for this new supervisor just disappeared."

- When positions were shuffled in her department, the customer service department manager of a major organization sent the following memo to her staff (names have been changed):

  Sue Smith, who has replaced Bernice Jones, should receive mail and calls from customers who were formerly Bernice's. Terry Mason, who will replace Sue Smith's former position, should receive all calls and correspondence that formerly belonged to Sue. Karen Arnold, who will replace Terry Mason's old position, should receive mail and calls that belonged to Terry. However (important to remember), Karen Arnold will still receive calls from customers in Region 4.

  All the mail that belonged to Karen should still be given to her, along with the mail that formerly was Terry Mason's. Karen will continue to receive her regular mail only until a rep has been found to fill her old position, with the exception of customers in Region 4 whose files she will still retain. Any mail for Linda Bains should be placed in the box marked "Sandy."

With the state of communication in the workplace in such a grim state, it's no wonder that nothing can help guarantee career security more than effective communication skills. Business communications expert

Dianna Booher points out in *Communicate with Confidence!* (McGraw Hill), "In survey after survey — from senior executives reminiscing about their career success to recruiters hiring college graduates — communication always tops the list of skills for success."

That's why — whether you're writing a memo to your boss, or calling a client for new business, or answering a complaint from a customer— improving your communication skills is the fourth simple thing you can do for your career today and tomorrow. Here are some suggestions you can begin applying now.

WHAT WOULD YOU DO?

GET A GOOD GRADE FOR GRAMMAR

A coworker recently criticized your grammar. It came as a surprise — Check your local bookstore for one of the excellent grammar workbooks now available. Review your workbook thoroughly, and do all the recommended exercises. Doing so will help you become familiar with the common usages that can cause problems for many people when it comes to grammar.

Here are a few more suggestions for improving your use of the English language:

- **Take a continuing education class in English at a local high school or university.** The regular routine of preparing for class, plus frequent quizzes to test your knowledge will help ensure that you'll learn the material.

- **Maintain a list of the grammatical errors you commonly make.** Write down the correct versions, review it regularly, and consciously try to use the correct forms.

- **Tune in to your colleagues' use of grammar.** Take note of their mistakes — and try not to make the same ones yourself.

- **Listen to usage and grammar tapes.** Play them just before bedtime and during your commute to and from work.

- **Don't be defensive when someone points out your grammar mistakes.** Instead, use their knowledge to your own advantage. Thank them for the feedback, then find out the correct usage — and make it part of your own "grammar bank."

- **Read and listen to the people who are paid to use language correctly.** Read the daily newspaper. Pay close attention to your TV news reporters and other well-educated (and well-spoken) individuals.

- **Keep a dictionary handy.** Use it to check out the meaning of any new words you hear. This will expand your vocabulary and help keep your interest in language alive.

ACTION IDEA

Try this mini-grammar quiz. Choose A or B:

1. (a) Everyone should bring their own note-books; or (b) Each person should bring their own notebooks

2. (a) I'm not sure where the memo is; or (b) I'm not sure where the memo is at

3. (a) Praise has a great effect on John; or (b) Praise has a great affect on John

4. (a) Mary and Sue will take care of this; or (b) Mary and her will take care of this.

In each case, (a) is the correct answer. Miss any? Check out a grammar book.

ARE GOOD COMMUNICATION SKILLS GOOD FOR YOUR HEALTH?

Mounting scientific evidence demonstrates that isolation and suppression of feelings often lead to illness, whereas intimacy and social support can be healing and promote good health. A recent report cited in *Prevention* magazine found that "social isolation is as significant to mortality rates as smoking, high blood pressure, high cholesterol, obesity, and lack of physical exercise." The study also showed that those with few or weak social ties were twice as likely to die as those with strong ties.

These conclusions underscore the need for the development of good communication skills as a way to promote social integration and better health.

The basic principle of good communication is that our feelings help to connect us, while our thoughts (particularly our judgments) tend to isolate us. Here are some ways to increase your ability to get close to others:

- Identify your feelings. Many people have a hard time distinguishing between a thought and an emotion. What are some common emotions? Anger, fear, worry excitement, and confusion. How about some common thoughts? "I am right; you're wrong," "You never listen," and "You did it again!"

- Express your feelings. Say how you feel, but try to express it as a feeling instead of a thought or a judgment. You don't necessarily have to tone it down, particularly if you're feeling a positive emotion. Express negative feelings in terms of yourself. Never cast blame with statements like "You always embarrass me." Rather, say, "I get embarrassed when people point out my weaknesses."

- Listen actively and compassionately. Knowing how to listen is as important as knowing how to express feelings. Read between the lines to determine the feelings behind what the other person says. Remember that other people want to be heard, just as you do.

- Acknowledge what other people say. You can express acknowledgment without necessarily agreeing. You might say, "I understand that you are angry because the report was late. But I am frustrated because two other jobs had pressing deadlines, too."

- Learn to say, "I want." Most of us are taught not to express ourselves so directly because it might sound selfish. But if you clearly and directly state your wants, others won't feel manipulated (as they would if you were less direct).

TEAMS' SECRET SUCCESS TOOL: COMMUNICATION

Sometimes it's tempting to hold back opinions and criticisms of fellow coworkers for fear it will destroy team spirit. "But honest communication delivered in nonthreatening ways can only make teams stronger," says Kelly Byrd, a Boston team counselor. Is your communication style helping or hampering your team's efforts? Ask yourself:

1. Am I willing to disagree with members of the team?

2. Do I listen attentively to all viewpoints while withholding judgment?

3. Do I recognize and praise team members for their ideas and suggestions?

4. Do I provide descriptive, specific, and helpful feedback to fellow team members?

5. Do I encourage team members to assess my strengths and weaknesses?

If you can say "yes" to all these questions, you're an effective team communicator. "Everyone has a different style of communication," says Byrd, "but the driving force of every successful team is honest, open discussion. Delivered with heart, it is the secret tool of every effective team."

BUILD RAPPORT — SUBTLY

Communication is more than a matter of words and expressions. The quality of your rapport with others, particularly customers, is a key factor in your success in connecting with them. "You talk to people to communicate with them," explains consultant George R. Walther, author of *Power Talking* (Berkley). "And that's done on two levels. Yes, there are facts and information to exchange. But first the doors of rapport have to open."

Rapport can be loosely defined as a feeling of sameness. "When we feel rapport with others, the channels are open, we're on the same wavelength," he says.

Some basic methods of building rapport are obvious to most of us, such as using the other person's name during the conversation, and showing an interest in the customer's viewpoint. But Walther identifies a second, more subtle route to gaining rapport: mirroring the other person's communication patterns.

To make rapport work, you first must understand that people think and express themselves in three different ways:

1. with visual images;

2. with feelings; and

3. with silent, internal "conversations."

Most people switch systems frequently, but one usually dominates, notes Walther.

Picking up on a caller's style, and then mirroring it back to him or her, shows that you're both on the same wavelength. Suppose, for example, the person you are speaking with says, "As I look at this, I see lots of confusion. Perhaps you can shed some light on a few points." To heighten your chances of being understood clearly and without resistance, you could respond, "Let's look at it from another angle and I'll see if I can create a clearer picture for you." You wouldn't say, "It sounds like you haven't heard what I'm talking about. Listen to it this way," because then you'd be talking on different channels, Walther explains.

"To build rapport, match the representational system used," says Walther. "You do this by listening carefully and then 'packaging' what you want to express before it travels from your mind to your mouth to their ears. Target each caller's representational system and your statements will be more readily digested."

Walther says effective communication is the result of continuous monitoring and adjustment: "True communication is getting the response you seek. If you aren't getting the response you want, change, adapt, and model your behavior after those with whom you wish to communicate. You'll open the door of rapport more quickly and communicate objective facts more clearly."

T-A-C-T-F-U-L Communication Tips

Tact. We all know who has it, and we've all been offended by those who seem to have a talent for saying the wrong thing. Tact is knowing the right thing to say in a given situation. It means knowing what to do or say to avoid giving offense and to help foster goodwill. Don Gabor, author of *Speaking Your Mind in 101 Difficult Situations* (Simon & Schuster), offers these tips for engaging in tactful conversation:

T = Think before you speak. Take a second or two to size up the situation and consider to whom you're talking.

A = Apologize quickly when you blunder. Don't fall all over yourself trying to make excuses, but acknowledge you're wrong with a touch of humility.

C = Converse, don't compete. People who "talk to win" tend to be tactless and boring because they see conversations as debates rather than a mutual exchange of information, ideas, opinions, and feelings.

T = Time your comments. Is the other person in a listening mode? Don't bring up sensitive or personal topics when either of you is upset or angry for instance. Knowing when to say something is as important as knowing how to say it.

F = Focus on behavior, not personality. Explain how the other person's behavior affects you and how you'd like it to change.

Action Idea

Today, begin making a conscious effort to eliminate words like should, ought to, and never. When speaking with coworkers and customers, they are almost always heard as judgments or criticisms. ("You should put that report on disk" versus "You can save a lot of space on your hard drive if you put that report on disk." "You ought to put your payment in the mail the first of the month" (versus "We're more likely to receive your payment by the due date if you post it on the first of the month").

U = Uncover hidden feelings. For example: "I appreciate your concern, but it sounds as if you're feeling angry about this. ..."

L = Listen for feedback. Poor listening skills often lead to tactless comments.

HANDS UP SUCCESS TALK

We're probably all familiar with that big-screen image of thoughtfulness and attentiveness: a person's hands coming together in the form of a steeple. Doctors and psychiatrists — at least in the movies — "steeple" their hands while listening to their patients. You too can project the image of deep thought and seriousness. Just steeple your hands when you're at meetings or while listening to colleagues one on one. The action will help convey your image as someone who's attentive to what others have to say.

TALK TIPS FROM TV TALK PRO

Want to be a success? Then learn to be a successful talker. That's the advice of talkmeister Larry King in *How to Talk to Anyone, Anytime, Anywhere: The Secrets of Good Communication* (with Bill Gilbert, Random House). The super-articulate host of CNN's *Larry King Live* identifies several characteristics shared by the best talkers he has encountered. All of them, King says:

- Have unique points of view, even on familiar topics.

- Are not only interested in or knowledgeable about what concerns them personally. They can think and talk about a wide range of issues and experiences.

- Show enthusiasm for what they do — and interest in what you're saying. King describes them as passionate about what they turn their minds to.

- Don't feel driven to always make themselves the center of attention. "They don't talk about themselves all the time," King emphasizes.

- Are blessed with curiosity, and freely ask "Why?" And when you talk, they want to hear more.

- Have the gift of empathy. They try to put themselves in your place in order to understand what you're saying.

- Share the gift of humor, and can laugh at themselves. King observes that the best conversationalists frequently tell stories on themselves.

- Don't try too hard, because they have confidence that their own style of speaking will work for them.

Try expanding your conversational skills by adapting one or more of the above characteristics. Who knows, maybe Larry King will be praising *your* conversational skills someday!

AVOIDING COMMUNICATION PITFALLS

Do you have trouble getting your message across to others? Do you misunderstand their messages? "Even if you were a perfect communicator, you would still find yourself beset with communication problems due to the fact that you have to deal with all of us other imperfect communicators," says management consultant Michael LeBoeuf.

Communicating successfully takes effort. But you can become a more effective communicator by becoming more aware of the problems and pitfalls of communication and by finding ways to overcome them.

In *Working Smart* (Warner Books), LeBoeuf offers these guidelines for strengthening communication:

1. Recognize the inadequacy of communication. "Communication is a complicated, symbolic, abstract process with an unlimited number of things that can go wrong and that usually do," he says.

2. Think existentially. "Remember that words are only symbols for reality in much the same way that maps represent territories," says LeBoeuf. "Frequently, things are not as they appear to be."

3. Find the total meaning in others' messages. "Don't just listen for words. Look for gestures, expressions, the sender's posture, and tone of voice," he advises. And be conscious of these things when you are the sender.

4. Consider the source. "Who delivers a message is usually at least as important as what is said," explains LeBoeuf. The better you know your communicator, the more accurately you can assess message and motive. LeBoeuf says this recommendation is often ignored. "It's a good rule of thumb to remember that people will tell you what they want you to hear," he says.

5. Ask questions. "A lot of confusion can be nipped in the bud by asking someone to repeat or rephrase their statement," LeBoeuf says.

6. Be specific. "Illustrate your point," he says. Don't say, "You're causing us to miss our deadlines." Instead, say, "By starting your assignment so late and not giving it the time it needs, you are making the rest of the team fall behind schedule."

7. Communicate in everyday language. Don't use big words when there's a simpler way to say it.

8. Don't be afraid to say "I don't know." Faking the answer only compounds the problems of ignorance.

9. Remember nonverbal communication. "Punctuality communicates. Body language communicates. And silence communicates," says LeBoeuf. "You may be inadvertently sending wrong messages."

10. Be tactful. "The Christmas party isn't the place to ask the boss for a raise," says LeBoeuf. "The location and frame of mind that you and the other party are in have a great deal to do with how well their ideas will be received and exchanged."

Finally, don't let all these communication concerns stress you out! "A relaxed, open attitude will make people more receptive to your ideas and willing to share their ideas with you," he says.

How Can I Misunderstand You? Let Me Count the Ways

Remember the game of "Telephone"? One person whispers a message to someone; that person passes it along to another; and so on. At the end of the game, the final recipient usually hears a far different — even hilarious — version of the original message.

No matter how careful you are in considering your words before you speak, there's always the chance your audience won't hear what you intend to say. The typical message is actually six messages:

- What you mean to say;

- What you actually say;

- What the other person hears;

- What the other person thinks was said;

- What the other person says;

- What you think the other person says.

When you're trying to communicate with a coworker, the message you intend to send will likely be interpreted as one of the other five. Make yourself as clear as possible and don't discourage questions.

Make Yourself Heard

How do you get people to listen to you?

- Get to the point — and stay there! If you take too long to say what you want to say, your listeners will become impatient. They may stop listening altogether or jump to the wrong conclusion.

- Restate your key point in another way to make sure it's getting across.

- Check for understanding. Ask if you've made yourself clear or if there are questions.

- Maintain credibility. People listen when they feel they can believe what you say. Don't exaggerate or "fudge" the facts.

TONGUE-TIED? OVERCOME A FEAR OF SPEAKING

Do you get tongue-tied and breathless just thinking about making a presentation? Thorough preparation is the key to overcoming this kind of fear, which afflicts millions of people. Here's what you can do:

- Deal with the physical symptoms of your fear. Drink lukewarm water to ease a dry throat, for example. Deep breathing before you speak will help you overcome a shaking voice and breathlessness. Count to seven or eight while breathing in, then start over and count the same while breathing out.

- Identify your fears during your presentation, and then rehearse how you would handle the situation.

- Practice your presentation to develop confidence in your knowledge and your ability to share it with others.

- Use positive self-talk by writing affirmations, such as "I'm a relaxed, confident speaker, and people are interested in what I have to say." Then repeat them to yourself several times a day.

Keep in mind that positive thinking alone won't resolve your insecurity. It must be combined with thorough preparation.

- Organize your material one more time the night before your presentation. You will sleep better if you know that everything is in order.

- Be the first to arrive in the room where you'll speak. You'll begin to relax as you settle in, distributing any handout materials, testing the microphone, and carefully setting up equipment.

Now start talking!

THE WRITE STUFF: MAKE IT EASY TO READ

"This looks easy to read — I'll go ahead and look it over right now." That's the kind of response you want when you write a document — whether it's a lengthy memo, a report or a proposal. "Otherwise your document may end up in the 'low priority' pile of items to read," notes Casey Hawley, a corporate trainer based in Atlanta, Georgia.

"Always make it easy for the reader," Hawley urges. "Use white space creatively, for instance. Scattering white space throughout your document makes it more inviting to the eye — and easier to read. Most of us have so much to read these days that we simply skim — or else skip altogether — a dense page of type."

Here are some tips for creating readable documents:

- Try double-indenting lists and allowing an extra line between short paragraphs. These techniques break up blocks of type with a little extra white space.

- Use boldface type for emphasis. "Most people just use bold to highlight names or headings," notes Hawley. "But it also can be used very effectively to draw the reader's eye and encourage him or her to keep reading the document." You can highlight words that are of special significance to your readers. These could include the names of items or equipment, or a phrase that relates to their mission statement (such as "excellence in service").

  "Use boldface type sparingly or you'll create monotony for the reader," advises Hawley. "Don't use more than one bold word or phrase per page — and don't use it on every page."

- Use bullets liberally. "Bullets used to be considered the tool of people who couldn't write proper sentences," Hawley observes. "Now bullets are essential in business documents to group lists of words or phrases in easily readable form or to crystallize key points you don't want the reader to miss."

- Write titles and headings from the reader's point of view rather than your own. This encourages people to read and retain the information in your document. So instead of "Transportation committees report on parking," for example, the title of your memo about new parking assignments might read, "What to do about parking."

- Consider using an appendix for support information. "People won't read every word — or even every page — of a long document," Hawley emphasizes. "But you want to encourage them to read at least far enough to get your main points. So put as much support information as possible — facts, figures, studies you're citing — in an appendix at the back of your document. Then readers don't have to wade through technical or dry material up front; they have the option of turning to the appendix for reference."

ABBREVIATE YOUR NOTE TAKING

If you take a lot of notes, or must decipher the boss's notes, common abbreviations can save you time. The *Take-Charge Assistant* newsletter lists these business abbreviations:

acv — actual cash value	hc — hard copy
aia — advise if available	i/o — instead of
aods — as of date specified	nd — no date
a/p — authority to pay	p/n — please note
bof — beginning of file	pto — please turn over
dos — date of sale	/s/ — signed
fka — formerly known as	sa — subject to approval
foc — free of charge	

ACTION IDEA

Make your documents easier to read by learning at least two new formatting techniques provided by your software. A few options that can add variety to your documents: A statement "box" in the middle of the page; different fonts for subheads; shaded headings (white letters on a black or dark gray background).

YOU CAN'T SCRAWL YOUR WAY TO SUCCESS

Good penmanship is still a quality job skill. In an age of computers and sophisticated word processing programs, handwritten notes have a human feel that goes a long way, especially in business. Your handwriting should be legible.

Consider some facts: According to the *Christian Science Monitor*, illegible handwriting costs U.S. companies $200 million a year and sabotages the effective exchange of information. Ninety percent of business executives complain about poor employee handwriting, the paper reports. What's more, 38 million illegibly addressed envelopes cost the U.S. Postal Service $4 million each year.

Good handwriting is essential for everything from notes and memos to signatures and customer orders. It's bad enough when a coworker has to ask you for clarification. But, when that person doesn't get clarification and makes an incorrect assumption as a result, the consequences can be much worse.

Mistakes made from an improperly interpreted business memo can have far reaching effects in your department or even the company, no matter how innocuous you may think your handwritten memo is.

So really think about everything that you write down — and what confusion could result if it were misread.

DON'T — I SAID DON'T — BE REDUNDANT!

Using redundancies — words and expressions that say the same thing twice — will undercut the effectiveness of your business correspondence. For example, you should use:

- finished, *not* absolutely finished;
- mix, *not* mix together;
- experience, *not* past experience;
- unique, *not* totally unique;
- total, *not* complete total;
- repeat, *not* repeat the same;
- file, *not* file away;
- consensus, *not* consensus of opinion;
- postpone, *not* postpone until later;
- essentials, *not* key essentials;
- disregard, *not* disregard completely;
- expert, *not* qualified expert.

AVOID THOSE 'ZINGER' MEMOS

"Zinger" memos can zing back and hurt your company and your career, says Joan Menninger, author of *The Perfect Memo* (Doubleday). Loaded or inflammatory language can be embarrassing and cause serious internal, external, or legal damage.

Whenever you're writing something critical, she says, a red light should flash in your brain. If you spot a company problem that needs immediate attention, for example, watch the wording of your "alert" memo.

Don't write: These crooks are robbing us blind. Instead, use a specific, factual statement that doesn't make or imply a judgment: We have severe shortages.

It's essential that memos report facts and don't place blame. Objectivity is critical, says Menninger. And every statement should be substantiated with evidence, either presented in the memo or on file.

QUICK TIPS

- **Unclog your speech.** Avoid phrases such as, "you know," "like," and "uh," which do nothing but dilute the impact of what you're saying. Peter Guiliano, president of the Executive Communication Group, Inc., suggests that an easy way to get rid of junk words and phrases is to record your side of a phone conversation and play it back later.

- **Accent the positive!** Are your conversations filled with negatives — words like "can't," "not," and "won't"? Coworkers, bosses, and customers will have a more positive impression of you if you highlight what you *can* do, accentuating "yes," "can," and "will."

- **Take call cues.** When making a phone call, listen to how the other person answers the phone. If the person says, "William Grimace speaking," it's a cue that he doesn't want to be called "Bill."

- **Help with names.** Ever had to call someone whose name you didn't know how to pronounce? Make the receptionist your ally. Say, "Hello, I'm trying to reach someone in Finance named Mary. ... It looks like I'm going to have a problem with this last name. Can you help me out, please?"

- **Check that pronunciation.** Proper pronunciation is a vital workplace skill. Start by making sure you know the proper pronunciation of all your company's products and services. Then use a dictionary to find the proper pronunciation of any other words you find yourself having trouble with.

- **Tone it down.** Pay attention to your tone of voice. For example, ending phrases on a high note can be interpreted as sarcasm. It's better to maintain a moderate tone of voice. Never speak too loudly, too softly, or with too much inflection.

QUIZ

'Why Can't I Speak Up?'

"I sometimes have an idea that I think would work well for our group. But something holds me back from speaking up. Later, someone else initiates the same idea, it's welcomed, and I feel miserable for keeping quiet."

— *S.B.J., Richmond, Virginia*

You need a boost in self-confidence. You give a lot of thought to problems at work, and your solutions are good ones. Take the following quiz to see if a simple lack of faith in yourself might be the problem.

	YES	NO
1. Do you feel successful on the job?	____	____
2. Do you feel successful in your life?	____	____
3. Under pressure, do you feel that things will work out?	____	____
4. If a coworker disagrees with you, do you see it as a simple difference of opinion that doesn't reflect on you?	____	____
5. Do you solve many of the problems in your department?	____	____
6. Do you take risks?	____	____
7. Do you get a full night's sleep, free of worry about work?	____	____
8. Do your friends make you feel good about yourself?	____	____
9. At meetings, are you more concerned about issues than about what impression you will make?	____	____
10. In adversity, do you hold on to positive emotions?	____	____
11. Most mornings, do you spring out of bed and look forward to the pleasures and challenges ahead of you?	____	____
12. Do you often feel there isn't enough time in the day to accomplish everything you'd like?	____	____
13. Do you set goals and constantly work to achieve them?	____	____

TOTAL NUMBER OF YES ANSWERS: _____

Your confidence quotient: Twelve to 13 YES answers indicate that you have a healthy level of self-confidence. You see disappointment as an isolated event rather than an overall indicator of the direction of your life. Eight to 10 YES answers indicate a moderate level of self-confidence. At times, you may not feel certain if your actions are going to produce the results you hope for. Seven or fewer YES answers indicate that you need to build your self-confidence. Spend some time each day focusing on your personal and professional successes. Be sure you eat right and get proper exercise. You'll begin to feel better about yourself inside and out, and you'll soon be speaking up more often.

YOUR CAREER SURVIVAL TAKE-AWAY

The 4th simple thing you *must* do to keep your job today (*and* tomorrow)

Develop your *powerful communication skills*

Good communication skills are one of the qualities most sought after by employers. Effective communication helps you get the information you need more quickly and accurately; builds credibility with customers and colleagues; improves teamwork; helps facilitate problem solving; and generally helps you put your best foot forward. Don't settle for the communication skills that come naturally for you. Your self-esteem will grow in direct correlation to your ability to communicate clearly and effectively in a variety of situations.

WHAT YOU CAN DO

- **Think before you speak or write.** Try to become aware of the various options open to you when someone accuses you, angers you, praises you, or motivates you. "Simply being aware of your options and ways to express those options will expand your communication horizons," says communications expert Dianna Booher.

- **Brush up on your grammar.** To a surprising degree, others judge you by how you speak. Making the effort to learn one new word a day can dramatically improve your vocabulary.

- **Pay attention to what others say and write.** What made you respond a particular way to a comment or a letter you received? How do you react to another person's good (or poor) vocabulary or grammar?

- **Slow down.** Before you send out that e-mail, take a deep breath and read it through one more time — slowly. Is it conveying the message you intended? Have you checked all spellings, including coworkers' names?

CHAPTER FIVE

Simple Thing #5:
BUILD *BETTER* RELATIONSHIPS WITH DIFFICULT PEOPLE

"Doesn't it seem some days as though other people were put in the world for no other reason than to aggravate you?"

— ED HOWE (1853-1937), AMERICAN JOURNALIST

INTRODUCTION

Do you know anyone at work who

- throws up roadblocks to slow you down or make you look bad?
- uses you as a scapegoat for their mistakes?
- shouts at you?
- undermines your decisions?
- backstabs?
- lies?
- verbally assaults you?
- threatens (or carries out) physical violence?

Congratulations — like the vast majority of working people, you have a difficult person or two to contend with. They may be a boss, a coworker, or a customer, but no matter who they are, their sole mission in life seems to make it a little less pleasant for everyone they contact.

Coping with difficult people at work is a bigger problem now than ever before. In the current work environment, where many are concerned with job security, difficult coworkers are in overdrive, trying to undermine others.

The good news is that by knowing the techniques to deal with difficult people, you can boost your confidence, improve your competence at work, reduce stress, and increase your enthusiasm and productivity. Management will respect you for your ability to handle difficult people, and that will make you more irreplaceable in your job today and tomorrow.

The topics covered in the following pages reveal that many kinds of difficult people exist. Studying the various coping techniques can help when you're forced to deal with a troublemaker. It's not so important to remember the exact words to use; focus instead on how to control your emotions and how you can respond to diffuse difficult situations without letting the difficult person keep the upper hand.

WHAT WOULD YOU DO?

WORKPLACE INSULTER VICTIMIZES COWORKERS

*Y*ou've had it! Someone you work with always slips subtle jabs and put-downs into your conversations. Sometimes he is cruel and makes "funny" comments at others' expense.

This type of person insults others for one reason — power. As long as you keep silent, you give him exactly what he wants, which is control over you and your colleagues. Productivity, morale, and self-esteem are all casualties of this brand of verbal assault. You're on the right track by not playing into the insulter's hand.

Such individuals are professional when it comes to comebacks — and they generally are not above retaliating. So, don't respond with an insult of your own. You will probably lose the battle. When someone at work hurls an insult your way, keep your composure. It's not easy, but the more relaxed you are, the less emotional you'll be. And you'll be able to address the situation logically. Don't fume silently. Instead, force yourself to look the person in the eye and respond to the insult directly: "That sounded like a putdown. Was it?"

Most people will back off, deny, or apologize for insulting behavior when confronted. At least you'll have given the person an opportunity to save face, even though he doesn't really deserve that brand of courtesy from you. But, that really makes you a much bigger person, doesn't it?

If, by chance, the person says it was indeed a jab, respond with: "That's too bad. I was hoping I was wrong." Insults lose their impact if they elicit little reaction. You might even ask, "What are you trying to say? Why would you say that?" Insulters prefer to hit and run. Most likely, this person will retreat if you press for an explanation and try to make him accountable. In short, insulters are often cowardly.

Make a pact with your coworkers that you won't be bothered by such drivel. Reinforce one another. That way, you'll take away the insulter's ammunition. Don't be surprised if it is a long time before this antagonist strikes again.

BATTLING THE OFFICE BULLY

Remember the schoolyard bully who waited in the shadows and threw your books into a puddle? Fortunately, most of us don't have to worry about being waylaid by physical bullies in the grown-up world. Instead, we contend with bullies who attack with putdowns and innuendoes.

"It's like being hit in the stomach with a fist of words," explains Suzette Haden Elgin, author of *The Gentle Art Of Verbal Self-Defense* (Marboro Books Inc.). "Verbal bullying is very much like physical bullying. Instead of physical force, language is used to inflict damage."

ACTION IDEA

The next time someone is nasty, turn the put-downs into jokes. Lillian Glass recommends memorizing a few great lines so they're on the tip of your tongue when you need them. They should have enough edge (without being cruel) to make the toxic person stop and think twice before taking you on again. For example, you could say, "Just keep on talking so I'll know that you're not thinking."

ACTION IDEA

Bullies succeed because they catch us off guard. Here's a chance to be prepared for the office bully's next attack. Below, write the most common form of the bully's attack ("You certainly take a lot of sick days." "Don't you answer your e-mail?"):

_____
_____
_____
_____
_____
_____
_____

Now draft the response you want to make:

_____
_____
_____
_____
_____
_____
_____

Rehearse and be ready with your response!

Forget the cliché about "sticks and stones." Says Elgin: "Words can hurt you." What can be done about an office bully? Here are some tactics:

- Confront the bully. Say: "I'm sorry you feel you have to do that, but I won't put up with that kind of behavior. It has no place here." It can be startlingly effective. "Bullies lack boundaries of their own behavior. Some external controls may force them to back off," explains Harry Levinson, Ph.D., a respected organizational psychologist and head of the Levinson Institute in Waltham, Massachusetts. Such a confrontation ought to be done in private. A bully is unlikely to back down in front of an audience.

- Don't take the bait. Every verbal attack has two parts, Elgin explains: the bait, which will always get you in trouble, and the real attack (the presupposition). Always respond to the real attack. For example, consider a bully who says, "If you really wanted to get ahead around here, you'd spend more time at your desk." If you respond by saying, "What do you mean? I'm at my desk working all day," you've fallen for the bully's bait.

What you should respond to is, "If you really wanted to get ahead ... ." Answer that presupposition by saying, "When did you start thinking I don't care about succeeding in the company?" By refusing to rise to the bait and responding neutrally to the real attack, you defuse your attacker and stop him in his tracks, says Elgin. It's not the expected reply. It will throw the bully off balance and save you from an argument.

- Specify the behavior that is unworkable. Say: "You can't just fire from the hip and demean me in front of others."

- Don't play armchair psychologist. You can't undo all the psychological history that has created this particular bully. Restrict the discussion to specific behaviors you can identify, not theories of motivation, advises Levinson.

- Don't let your performance suffer. Recognize that you are not causing the bully's behavior. Remember: You don't have to let a bully ride herd over you and make your life at work miserable.

Finally, don't fall into the victim role, warns Elgin. Most victims don't realize that their reactions feed and encourage bullies. "Step away from the problem so you can analyze it and squelch it calmly before it gets truly out of hand," she recommends.

OH, THOSE MEAN, NASTY PEOPLE!

Some people are just downright nasty. They show no restraint when it comes to making insulting comments. They go around all day being unpleasant and difficult. And, unfortunately, their nasty attitude takes a toll on everyone who has to coexist with them.

The good news is that you no longer have to be victimized by such people. Never self-destruct over individuals whose behavior is basically toxic. That's the advice of Lillian Glass, Ph.D., author of *Toxic People: 10 Ways of Dealing With People Who Make Your Life Miserable* (Simon & Schuster).

The key, says Glass, is to gain physical control over your emotions when dealing with toxic people. You can do this with the tension-blowout technique. It will help you take in oxygen and release carbon dioxide, countering the stressful physical state that literally makes you feel sick. Here's how to blow out tension:

- Breathe in deeply through your mouth.
- Hold your breath for three seconds as you think about the toxic person.
- Blow him or her right out of your system with a mighty exhalation of air.
- Repeat the procedure until you get that person's negativity completely out of your system. Then take a deep breath of fresh, untainted air.

WATCH OUT FOR PERILOUS TEAM PERSONALITIES!

Learning to work with coworkers is part of being a conscientious team member. Sure, you can choose to deal with challenging personalities in ego-satisfying ways, such as speaking your mind or ignoring anyone who bothers you. But such approaches usually cause more problems. A side effect is that you inadvertently increase your own stress. No one is worth that price.

Here are healthy methods for dealing with three troublesome personalities, recommended by Juliet Nierenberg and Irene S. Ross, authors of *Women and the Art of Negotiating* (Simon & Schuster):

- The spoiler. This person finds fault with everything. His focus is typically on problems, but never on solutions. Most likely, he is sour and critical of coworkers. To deal with this personality effectively, document all agreed-upon points with witnesses. When working together on a project, watch how you phrase ideas. Spoilers look for the loophole. Best defense: optimism.
- The pressure cooker. This person is typically aggressive, loses her temper, and likes getting the upper hand, even if it means embarrassing others. It's tough to keep cool in the face of a pressure cook-

ACTION IDEA

Don't allow a difficult team member to spoil your team's spirit.

• Does a difficult team member fit one of the three personalities?

• Which personality type is this person (spoiler, pressure cooker, bulldozer)?

_____

• To help bring this person under control at your next meeting, you will

_____
_____
_____

• If that action isn't enough, you will

_____
_____
_____
_____

er. When she loses control, excuse yourself until the situation cools down. When confrontations are mild, maintain eye contact and a firm stance. Remember that the pressure cooker explodes to gain or maintain control. Listen, don't argue. Best defense: deal unemotionally with the facts.

- The bulldozer. This person is a coward in disguise. He seeks out the weak spots in others, takes on a superior attitude, and never admits wrongdoing. Keep close wraps on your own weaknesses. When psychological pressure is applied (to either give in or assume blame), hold your own. Be clear about your objectives and maintain a calm, interested position. Best defense: friendly, logical resistance.

With all three of these negative coworkers, remember: you *can* control your reactions.

DEFUSING A WALKING POWDER KEG

Walking powder kegs — those coworkers or bosses with explosive tempers — can make life at work difficult.

If you allow it, this kind of person has you right where he wants you. He has an expressive talent to manipulate you with the threat of confrontation. Generally, most of us would prefer to keep our distance rather than engage in a skirmish with a short-fused coworker. After all, who likes to be caught off guard by a tempestuous colleague?

As long as you remain wary of him, he will remain quite comfortable with his control over you. Even managers have been known to avoid employees who overreact, so these powder kegs get away with murder. Others would rather make allowances or excuses for the powder keg than correct, criticize, or confront. If you look closely, you might even discover that your fuming coworker enjoys certain advantages that others don't.

These testy coworkers put their needs and wants first. They may scare others off due to a fear of criticism and/or because they are insecure. Often, they feel persecuted by coworkers, the company, and even society. They use defensiveness to keep others at bay. So, how do you deal with this kind of coworker?

Something must change if you want to be happier on the job. First, you don't want to get on the knee-jerk defensive. He will probably shout you down. As a result, you'll get flustered and angry and your work will suffer. Instead, work hard to change your reaction. Each of your teammates can calmly make it clear that you consider his behavior inappropriate. If he wants to discuss an issue with you, he'll have to do it without his typical approach. Make a pact that you'll all uphold a no-tolerance policy

His reaction will probably be explosive. Walk away from it. The more you acknowledge it, the more he'll use his temper. If you must discuss something with him, be tenacious by standing firm (and calm), letting his ridiculous tantrum run its course. And then proceed.

If you happen to be his boss, you have a responsibility to your other employees. Explain that you can't tolerate this type of behavior and that you won't grant special treatment because of it. Document your conversation for his personnel file.

RIGHT AND WRONG WAYS TO MANAGE CONFLICT

When properly managed, conflict can promote creativity, lead to better decisions, and initiate beneficial change within your team structure. Conflict is managed — although not always successfully — in varying ways:

- **"My way ... or the highway."** This is a "win-lose" strategy. The winner proves she has more power than the other and can force the loser to accept any solution. At best, a forced solution gains no enthusiasm or commitment to the principles of the winning side.

- **"We're one big happy family."** Smoothing over conflicts may involve securing a mutual "kiss and make up" strategy for the good of the department or team. But if this strategy does little to resolve the real causes of the conflict, it seldom leads to an effective, long-term solution.

- **"I don't want to talk about it."** Withdrawal or avoidance is wise when tempers get so hot that reason evaporates. But conflicts should be addressed at a later time, and this takes a cool head.

- **"Let's compromise."** A well-designed compromise benefits all parties and reduces hostility. But it doesn't guarantee that future conflicts will not develop. A compromise works only if coworkers trust one another.

The best solutions involve addressing and discussing with your teammates the actual causes of the problems. Effective resolution produces no losers and reduces the chances for future conflict. Here are some guidelines to manage conflict effectively:

- **Confront the opposing party.** Sidestepping issues or merely alluding to them only adds fuel to the fire.

- **Examine biases.** Before addressing a conflict, put aside personal prejudices. Then, you can keep these biases from interfering with issues.

- **Get personal feelings up front.** Often, issue-oriented conflicts are heightened because of personality problems. This often overlooked variable can remain long after an issue is resolved and become the basis for new conflict.

- **Minimize status differences.** Agree on a neutral site for a discussion, such as a meeting room. Using status or seniority as leverage in team conflicts leads to coercive compliance, not resolution.

- **Eliminate blame.** Fixing blame serves no useful purpose and only breeds defensiveness.

- **Don't hold out too long.** Rigidity can be a stumbling block. Smart communicators know when to push harder to gain more ground — and when to be flexible.

- **Identify mutual agreement.** No doubt, you and your teammates agree on something. For example, you have to agree that a conflict exists to take steps to resolve it. If you agree on the causes, you can develop workable solutions.

DIFFICULT CALLERS ARE PEOPLE, TOO! (YEAH, RIGHT)

Ranting and raving. Scheming and screaming. Difficult customers think they are more likely to negotiate solutions to their problems by making a fuss. In reality, they make the process more difficult.

The key to successfully handling difficult customers is to separate the person from the problem, says Roger Fisher, who teaches negotiation at the Harvard Law School. "Everyone knows how hard it is to deal with a problem without people misunderstanding each other, getting angry or upset, and taking things personally," Fisher says in his book, *Getting to Yes, Negotiating Agreement Without Giving In* (Penguin), co-authored with William Ury.

Your goal must be the same with any customer: to reach an agreement that is fair and acceptable both to the customer and to your company. "Keep in mind customers are always people first," Fisher explains. "Failing to deal with others sensitively as human beings prone to human reactions can be disastrous." Here's what to do:

- Recognize and understand the customer's emotions. Allow the customer to let off steam.

- Use symbolic gestures. Says Fisher: "Any lover knows that to end a quarrel the simple gesture of bringing a red rose goes a long way." The same holds for customers. A simple "I'm sorry you've had a problem" — spoken without placing blame — can reduce hostilities.

- Listen actively and acknowledge your customer's comments.

- Help the customer to share in solving the problem. Don't dictate a solution. Seek the customer's advice by asking, "What do you think would be the best solution?" Explains Fisher: "The feeling of participation is perhaps the single most important factor in determining whether a proposal will be accepted."

The bottom line: "Deal with people as human beings," he says. "Then you can go on to deal with the problem on its own merits."

'I'M BEING TRANSFERRED — *AGAIN?!*'

Customers often have unreasonable expectations when it comes to problem solving. They like — and often expect — immediate resolution of complaints. That's not always possible.

Suppose a customer calls with a billing problem. Thanks to staff downsizing, the customer may have been on hold longer than ever before. Technology can aggravate the situation. By the time you get on the line, a caller might have been holding for several minutes. Or he may have been transferred once or twice. The last thing callers want is another transfer.

If you must transfer the call, be sure to explain why — and offer sympathy. Say something like: "I know you've already been transferred a number of times. I will stay on the line to make sure your call reaches someone in billing and see that your questions are answered quickly."

Also, work out an arrangement with someone in billing in whom you have confidence. Then you can tell customers: "I'm going to refer this to Marianne in billing. She's very competent, and I'm sure you'll find her a pleasure to deal with."

This response personalizes the billing department. You'll give the caller an actual name and help eliminate any fear he has about getting lost in the loop.

When a customer still resists being transferred, try this: "Your problem can be handled more quickly by talking directly to billing, but I can understand your reluctance to be transferred. If you answer a few questions, I can put you on hold while I look into this for you." If you sense that the caller is becoming seriously aggravated by being on the phone so long, ask if you can have someone from billing call the customer back. Offer to write down detailed information about the customer's account so the person in billing will have an answer when he or she calls the customer.

If you take this kind of action, however, be sure to follow through and see that someone in billing actually does get back to the customer as promised. Otherwise, you and your company will be in even more hot water.

ARE YOU A DIFFICULT PERSON 'ENABLER'?

Sam Deep and Lyle Sussman, authors of *What to Say to Get What You Want* (Addison-Wesley), point out that it's necessary to consciously avoid taking on the role of "enabler" with difficult people. They observe that, by tolerating difficult people, we may be indirectly encouraging — or enabling — them to continue their bad behavior.

Here are some of their suggestions for preventing this:

- Avoid making empty threats. When you can't or won't carry through on a threat, the other person is even further encouraged to continue with the same behavior. If you say, for example, "I'll report what you've done," you'd better do so. When you make a threat, you must intend to carry it out, have the resources to do so, and then take action if there's no response.

- Don't protect troublesome individuals from the consequences of their behavior. Don't agree not to report the problem "this time" because you feel sorry for your coworker. And avoid keeping the problem entirely to yourself to protect the individual from getting a bad name within the organization. Your attempts to protect your problem coworker will only make it easier for that person to continue his unproductive behavior.

- Avoid making excuses for problem behaviors. Deep and Sussman acknowledge that we "seem to be losing some of the will in our society to hold people accountable for their behavior. When we make excuses for unacceptable behavior, the perpetrator feels, 'They're right; I'm not responsible for my actions.'" Do the trouble-maker on your team a favor and don't ever provide rationalizations for the way he acts.

- If you think you may be an "enabler" to your problem coworker, ask yourself why. Do you enable other difficult people in your life? Do you really want them to change? Complex psychological reasons may explain why any of us become enablers. One possibility, say Deep and Sussman, is that we want to keep the other person dependent on us in some way. Our willingness to tolerate and even unconsciously encourage bad behavior may also be due to the simple fact that we sometimes like to be the martyr or savior.

ADAPT YOUR CONFLICT STYLE

"When you're skilled at using different conflict styles, you're well-equipped to handle conflict resolution," says Sherry Boecher, a trainer with National Seminars Group, in Overland Park, Kansas. "But we all know people who always react the same in a conflict, regardless of whether their reaction is appropriate."

For example, Mary tends to "blow up" whenever someone strongly disagrees with her. And when anyone objects to that behavior, coworkers defend her: "Oh, well, that's just Mary." They give the stamp of approval to her conflict style, so she doesn't change.

Why should she?

Here are Boecher's suggestions for resolving conflict in an appropriate and productive way:

- **Domination.** Avoid dominating a conflict — unless it's the only way to resolve it. "Sometimes you may need to take control when things get out of hand in a conflict," Boecher observes. If a telephone caller is screaming into the receiver over a service problem, for example, you may need to dominate to gain control.

In this case, Boecher says, the "broken record" technique is best: "Mr. Stevens, I want to hear what you have to say but not this way. Please lower your voice or I'll have to hang up." Keep repeating.

Otherwise, domination is not an appropriate way to resolve conflict. Says Boecher: "There's a winner and a loser when you battle it out."

- **Compromise.** "When parties in conflict agree to compromise, they settle the dispute by each being prepared to give up something," Boecher points out. To get an extra hand to help on a major project, for example, your work team may need to agree to meet an earlier deadline. "Compromise is never inappropriate if the needs of both sides are being met in some way," she adds. "And when there's a crisis, or for some other reason it's important to reach an agreement quickly, compromise is the best solution."

- **Collaboration.** When possible, collaborate to solve a problem. "Together, the conflicting parties identify the issues, establish goals, and lay out an action plan for resolution," Boecher explains. This strategy is appropriate if you have time to pursue it, she says, but it's not usually effective in a crisis where time is of the essence.

Set ground rules for compromising and collaborating. Boecher advocates three:

1. No personal attacks or accusations.

2. No profanity.

3. Everyone will speak and be heard.

- **Self -disclosure.** In a heated conflict, use the technique of self-disclosure to talk about the key issues without offending the other parties. Focus on the facts and discuss how you feel about what happened: "When I am called names, I feel angry because I don't feel I'm being treated professionally or with respect." Try to avoid personal comebacks to attacks, such as "Don't you ever speak to me that way again!"

All three forms of conflict resolution have advantages and disadvantages, but are not appropriate in each situation. Choose your conflict management style carefully.

RESOLVING DIFFERENCES

When working relationships break down and expectations are unmet, misunderstandings surface. Tension in the workplace builds for those involved in these situations. What can you do to resolve these problems?

"Although uncomfortable, these troublesome situations are the new classrooms that can help us identify our needs and develop the skills we are missing," says Faith Ralston, Ph.D., in *Hidden Dynamics* (AMACOM). "These conflicts provide us with the opportunity to move beyond our current level of understanding," says Ralston. "There are three steps to the process of resolving differences."

Those three steps are:

1. Seek ground level. Understand that the other person's needs are as important as yours. Describe the incident or behavior that concerns you, and listen to the other person's point of view. Then, summarize both viewpoints. Do not try to resolve the problem yet, but do try to convey how each of you felt as a result of what occurred.

2. Look at the task. Make a decision on the priorities and actions needed. Discuss the work at hand and reach agreement on everything that needs to be done. At this point, you must only talk about the work that you need to do together, not the relationship.

3. Make it up. Return to the relationship and make decisions on how you will work together. It is important in this step to make agreements that are simple and easy to implement.

Give yourselves time to try out and assess the new behaviors. Continue to touch base about how things are working. It will help you refine and modify as you go.

WHEN A COWORKER WON'T HELP OUT

Sometimes getting a coworker to *go* along is tougher than getting him or her to *get along.* It's a situation we've all encountered. You need a coworker to do something he doesn't want to do. You've been turned down before, and you wouldn't ask if you didn't have to.

We've all had to make unpopular requests. The next time you need to get a coworker to "go along":

- Be pleasant. Only bosses have the authority to mandate that certain work be done. Being curt ensures a turndown.

- Avoid command-type language. Some people will establish a barrier when they hear words like must and have to.

- Respect opposing views. Respect the other person's point of view, even if it differs dramatically from yours.

- Find reasons for the refusal. Is this person really resisting or just trying to see how serious you are? Some people automatically refuse requests until they understand the need.

- Consider alternatives. If rebuffed, ask: "How could I change my request to make it acceptable?"

- Be resilient. If you don't get your way, don't leave in a huff. Retain your professional image for the next request.

- Make it an issue. If the long-term payoff seems worth it, go to your boss, explain the problem, and suggest a meeting to resolve it.

SULLEN COWORKER EMPLOYS PASSIVE RESISTANCE

Does this description describe anyone in your workplace? This type of coworker won't get involved in any workplace activities. He holes up in his office, does a minimum of work, and is always sulking. But when asked if anything is wrong, this coworker says that everything is fine. His behavior distracts your group and makes you feel self-conscious, as if you've done something wrong.

A passive resister can drive coworkers crazy because they make everyone feel they are somehow to blame for the sullenness this coworker exhibits. Generally, recluses feel that they're victims of some injustice, either by coworkers or the company. And they take it out on others. Rather than quitting to take another job, they feel a personal satisfaction in sticking around, annoying others, and throwing coworkers off balance. It seems that, no matter what you might say, the die has been cast, and you pay the price.

As a result, you and your colleagues probably avoid interaction with him because of the discomfort you feel. This just gives the passive resister more grist for his mill. And he gains a certain degree of power just by being silent.

Apparently this tactic works for some, although it's hardly the best way to work together because you cannot count on this coworker for help. Or can you? Try to engage this type of coworker more actively in the work you all do. Since you're not a boss, you cannot mandate his involvement. But you can solicit him for help.

Take a mental inventory of his strengths — areas in which he can truly offer some expertise. Then, ask him to assist you in solving a problem. For example, say: "I am stuck on this problem, and I know that you know a lot about this."

You might be able to achieve two goals. First, you'll give him some power by appreciating his expertise. Second, you might then compel him to take a more useful, active role in departmental issues.

WHY YOU DON'T WANT TO BE THE OFFICE ANN LANDERS

It's not that you don't want to be friendly.

But what do you do about a coworker who keeps coming to you with her personal problems.

You should not get personally involved with this coworker. Too often, people get caught between the proverbial rock and a hard place when it comes to friendships with coworkers. They want to be a supportive colleague but they find themselves being taken advantage of. It's hard to say "No" to someone who seems to need help so desperately. But, too often, once you try to help a coworker with a personal problem, he or she relies too much on you thereafter. This can have a negative impact for several reasons.

First, you say she depresses you with her personal problems. That not only affects you personally, but it probably affects the work you do, too. Your enthusiasm and efficiency suffer, particularly if she discusses personal matters. That doesn't make you look good to the boss.

You've been made to shoulder her burden, which adds to your stress. Most of us have plenty to worry about in our own lives without adding others' problems to the list.

Second, you can't really solve her problems. Although your advice may be sound, it might not work for your coworker. If that happens, guess who will get the blame? And that's not fair to you.

You're making a mistake if you just bear with this problem. Your needy coworker will continue to drag you down by seeking more advice. Nor should you deliberately try to alienate her. After all, you don't want to add to her misery.

Your goal should be to point her in the right direction. You might emphasize that you care about her personally but are not qualified to give the advice she needs. You could ask her questions that can lead her to make her own decisions. But if the problem is severe enough, she probably needs professional counseling.

You can offer to help her find someone who is qualified to help. (Your organization may have an employee assistance program.) Then, let the professionals take it from there. You can still be supportive without getting too involved.

TABOO TALK

Most people know discussing politics and religion is off-limits in the workplace. "By mutual consent, we avoid raising these subjects," says Kristin Anderson, author of *Knock Your Socks Off Answers* (AMACOM). "It's an unspoken social contract designed to smooth the waters of daily conversation, especially in work settings where we generally don't feel free to express personal views.

"In your personal life, you may feel free to agree or disagree with others' opinions," says Anderson. "But on the job, when the focus is on serving customers, disagreeing is risky, and agreeing can land you in the middle of an extended conversation that is irrelevant to your service task."

So how can you find a way out when presented with comments and questions about religion, politics, or other "hot" topics? When the topic is religion, Anderson offers this advice: "For the sake of customer service, you can acknowledge the good intentions without acknowledging the religious view behind them or encouraging further conversation.

"Your goal is to close the discussion and redirect the conversation to an appropriate topic as quickly and as simply as possible," she says.

For example, if a caller asks, "Are you saved?" you might respond with, "Thank you. How might I help you today?"

When the topic is politics, your answer should not agree, disagree, insult, or make an issue out of anything. "Just redirect the conversation and move on," suggests Anderson. For example, if a customer says, "I can't understand why anyone would have voted that clown into office, can you?" respond with, "That's politics. How may I help you today?"

Difficult issues and personal values do have a place in life, but on the job they only distract us from providing excellent service, says Anderson.

QUICK TIPS

- **Tough love for chatterboxes.** Explain to a chatty coworker that a long conversation takes up two persons' valuable time and that you are simply too busy to engage in conversation. Be kind, but direct. Also, point out that a person must be considerate of others who may be too polite to ignore the conversation. Offer to talk at break or lunch time.

- **Find a neutral zone.** If you have difficulty getting along with a coworker, search for a common ground: such as sports, a television show, or a hobby. Emphasize your similarities to chip away at the hard edges of your relationship.

- **Return to sender.** Vent your frustration at a difficult customer or coworker by writing her a letter. Spell out exactly how you feel. Then tear up that letter! You'll feel better and no further harm will be done.

- **Whatever you say.** Take the punch out of a coworker's disparaging remarks by simply agreeing with everything he says. For example, a comment like, "You've worn that same suit three times this week!" would get a response like, "That's right. I've worn this same suit three times this week." That will stop them in their tracks!

- **'You're kidding, right?'** When a customer tries to pressure you into doing something unethical, say no — but gently. Assume the customer must be joking and say so: "Oh, you know I couldn't do *that!*" Most likely, the customer will take the hint and drop the crazy request.

- **Turn team *no* to team *yes*.** If there are team members who say "No, no, no" to every idea that's proposed, put them in charge of finding alternatives to which they, and the rest of the team, can say, "Yes, yes, yes!"

QUIZ

Do Coworkers 'Guilt' You into Action?

"Sometimes I think I get suckered into doing things for coworkers that I don't want to do. A few of my coworkers have a talent for making me feel guilty, so I comply — only to feel angry later."

— P.B.W., Fond du Lac, Wisconsin

Guilt is one of the oldest forms of persuasion. Generally, it is synonymous with manipulation by capitalizing on others' personal weaknesses. Often, we actually allow ourselves to feel guilty. How susceptible are you to guilt-inducing tactics? Take the following quiz to find out. Answer each question YES or NO, then score yourself below.

	YES	NO
1. When you say no, do you feel you have to rationalize it?	____	____
2. When you comply with a request, do you often wish you were doing something else?	____	____
3. When someone expresses disapproval, do you automatically assume you're the one at fault — even when you aren't?	____	____
4. Are you inclined to apologize for circumstances that really have nothing to do with your actions?	____	____
5. When you feel guilty, do you have a tendency to overcompensate to make amends?	____	____
6. Do you get emotionally involved with your coworkers' problems?	____	____
7. Would you regard yourself as a "soft touch" when someone relates a problem?	____	____
8. Are you inclined to try and "fix" other people's problems for them?	____	____
9. Is it relatively easy for others to make you feel bad about yourself?	____	____
10. Do you fear that others won't like you if you say no — even to unreasonable requests?	____	____

Does guilt motivate you? There's no such thing as a guilt-free existence. However, the more NO answers you have, the better you cope with guilt. A low number of NO answers suggests you're a pushover. The resulting resentment you might feel can get you into trouble later. It's up to you to decide whether or not guilt will get the best of you.

YOUR CAREER SURVIVAL TAKE-AWAY

The 5th simple thing you *must* do to keep your job today (*and* tomorrow)

Build better *relationships with difficult people*

At one time or another, everyone has to deal with irate, rude, impatient, or aggressive people in the workplace. Handling difficult people requires understanding their different personality types. Once you know their motivation, you can call on the appropriate communication skill that will help diffuse tensions calmly. Consider this: Difficult people can actually be an asset to your professional growth; diffusing difficult situations shows you display grace under pressure and can work well with *all* kinds of people. That's a characteristic of a true job survivor.

WHAT YOU CAN DO

- **Make sure your accomplishments are well known to your boss and others in authority.** That way, if a coworker is trying to take credit for your work, you'll be protected against their attack.

- **Don't underestimate the value of humor.** If you can laugh off a snide remark, you'll show that you won't take the troublemaker's bait. Difficult people only succeed if you respond with anger.

- **This doesn't mean you should let inaccurate accusations or comments go unchallenged.** Confront the individual in private and in a quiet manner.

- **Learn to work around someone who continually puts up roadblocks.**

- **Do a lot of listening.** When you contend with difficult customers, they need time to blow off steam. Hear out the problem. But don't linger on what was wrong. Apologize if you're in the wrong. Then quickly find a solution.

CHAPTER SIX

Simple Thing #6:
MOTIVATE OTHERS TO GIVE *THEIR* BEST

*"Keep away from people who try to belittle your ambitions.
Small people always do that, but the really great make you feel
that you, too, can become great."*

— MARK TWAIN (1835–1910), AMERICAN AUTHOR

INTRODUCTION

How successful you are at work is judged by many factors, such as how well you perform your job and how you continue to grow and develop in your career. Then there are the factors you have no control over: mergers and layoffs and downsizing.

However, one area in which others judge your performance that may seem to be beyond your control is how well your coworkers do their jobs.

It may seem unfair to judge you for how well others do. After all, unless you are a manager or supervisor, you have little control over whether your coworkers show up for work, meet their deadlines, and produce quality work. But unless you're a hermit and work entirely on your own, you have daily contact with others. And, your actions and your expectations influence their attitudes and the work they produce.

- When you work hard to do your best each day, you influence your coworkers by your example.

- When you expect only the best from others, you influence them with your positive attitude and leadership abilities.

Expecting the best from others strengthens your career path because you will never achieve your own potential by accepting anything less. With your positive and supportive attitude, you give others confidence to strive for excellence.

The five first "7 Simple Things You *Must* Do for Your Job Today (*And* Tomorrow)" focus on how you can improve *your* communication and productivity skills. Simple Thing # 8 — Motivating Others to Do Their Best — carries your development to the next level, showing you techniques and skills that will help you bring out the best in *others*.

The results for your department or team: teamwork and quality work that everyone can be proud of. The results for you? The satisfaction of seeing others reach their potential and the opportunity to strengthen your leadership and motivational skills.

WHAT WOULD YOU DO?

MOTIVATING COWORKERS YOU DON'T LIKE

You must work closely with two coworkers you don't get along with. But, for your personal satisfaction (and career success), you don't want your personal feelings to prevent you from increasing motivation and productivity.

You don't have to like everyone you work with, but in this case, you must be able to work with them well enough to accomplish your goals. The solution? Change your attitude. "You have to have some sort of positive relationship, some level of comfort," advises career consultant Diane Blumenson.

The first step is commitment to a change of mind. Don't worry that your attempts to change the situation will seem insincere. If you're really committed, your efforts to improve the relationships will be welcomed, at least eventually.

To make progress, Blumenson suggests:

- **Don't overdo it.** At first, just be friendly and polite as opportunities present themselves.

- **Be positive.** You might have hated talking to these people before, but now talk about upbeat topics: the rewards you'll all receive for doing a good job.

- **Interact more frequently.** Finally, create your own opportunities for interaction. Soon, you'll at least be working effectively with one another and doing the job.

JUMP-START YOUR TEAM

Your team is doing okay but you want to be outstanding. What should you do? Pennsylvania-based organizational consultant Suzanne Zoglio says that a key ingredient to invigorating a team is to set goals.

"You've got to have a target, so you can aim for a bullseye," says Zoglio. "Too many teams shoot first, then draw a circle around what they've hit. But that's not motivating or refueling for a team."

But there are techniques that can help. Zoglio, author of *Teams at Work* (Tower Hill Press), offers these additional methods:

1. Take risks. No one feels motivated when new ideas aren't cultivated and encouraged. "Team members should know that it's okay to stick their necks out," says Zoglio. "Create a climate where the team has no reason to fear creativity."

2. Praise teammates who take risks. Team members will maintain a high level of motivation when they've had positive reinforcement in the past. "When someone offers a far-out idea, praise the person for their original thinking," says Zoglio. "When someone takes an unpopular position, praise their courage to 'swim

upstream.' When your teammates risk looking foolish by asking questions, praise their willingness to clarify a point for the team."

3. Keep quiet! When some coworkers do all the talking, others don't have an opportunity to open up. This stifles their motivation. One technique Zoglio recommends is to hand out three paper clips to each team member. When you speak, take one of your paper clips away. Then don't speak again until every other team member has spoken and turned in one paper clip. This helps ensure that everyone contributes.

4. Show results. "How did your team's last great idea impact the organization? How much money was saved? How many accidents were prevented?" asks Zoglio. When you recognize the impact your contributions make as a whole, you will be inspired to greater heights of innovation.

5. Accent the W.I.I.F.M. ("What's in it for me?") factor. Team members' contributions also have an impact on themselves. Ask yourself and your teammates what they've personally experienced from contributing in the past.

"Responses will be personal and varied," she says. "For some team members, the reward is knowing they have had the opportunity to utilize their talents. For others, it may be satisfaction from learning something new."

So, the next time your energy level needs a boost, remember what your hard work means to your team, your organization, and yourself.

HITTING YOUR COWORKERS' MOTIVATIONAL HOT BUTTONS

If you think motivating your team should be management's job, you're not alone. Many people spend a good part of their careers waiting for someone else to energize and excite them about their jobs. If they're lucky, they'll find a strong management figure who understands the importance of motivation. But they're just as likely to encounter a boss who cares only that the work gets done and not about how employees feel while doing it or if their motivational levels remain high.

For that reason, you and your teammates must take a proactive role in motivating your team to reach for the stars and have fun while you're getting there. Start by asking yourself the following questions to determine your current state of mind.

These questions can help identify individual motivational "hot buttons," reports business trainer and author Mark Sanborn in his book, *Team Built* (Master Media Books):

- What do you like most about your job?
- What do you like least about your job?
- What would you like to do in the future?

- When do you do your best work?
- Whom do you work best with?
- What gives you the most pride in your work?

"Answers to these questions help identify the diversity of values, wants, and desires within a team and provide the information necessary to tailor motivation to individuals," says Sanborn.

RECOGNITION SPURS TEAMMATES TO NEW HEIGHTS

Everyone performs better when given reinforcement, and coworkers are no exception. But in a work-team situation, the most important feedback doesn't come from management.

"In a team environment, peer reinforcement is more important than boss reinforcement," says Ken Keller, partner in The Carroll-Keller Group. Why? Because it is not a team member's job to provide feedback, whereas a boss is expected to give it. Peer reinforcement encourages repetition of positive behaviors and prevents negative ones from recurring, thus creating an environment that fosters dedication to the team and its efforts.

So, once you've decided to use reinforcement, how do you implement it? The critical step is learning what constitutes effective positive reinforcement. According to Keller, positive reinforcement is:

- Specific. When complimenting a team member on a job well done, be as specific as possible about what he or she did right. Saying, "Hey, you're really great," will not produce the same effect as saying, "Your suggestion to change the stations on the production line saved us $300 on the Phillips order. Great thinking!" As Keller pointed out, "A cursory pat on the back does little to bring back behavior we want to see again."

- Immediate. Any time lag rapidly diminishes the value of positive reinforcement. It's best to tell a team member that you appreciate his or her idea as soon as possible so that the situation and the suggestion are still fresh in both your minds. The immediacy will also help you be specific about the details of the idea or action. A compliment that comes too late seems like an afterthought.

- Achievable. Any recognition should be based on the person's own ability to achieve, rather than on a set standard. If a team member does something unusual or exceptional, that's the time to offer praise.

- Intangible. Reinforcement should always be as intangible as possible. For instance, if you reward someone with money for a good idea one time, but only with praise the next, he or she may feel that the second idea was second-rate. Or, teammates may begin to equate the worth of their rewards with the value of their ideas. "The more tangible the reinforcement is," Keller said, "the more

ACTION IDEA

Jessica Kittrell of Fayetteville, North Carolina, offers this idea for making coworkers feel appreciated and welcome. "At our monthly staff meetings, we celebrate all birthdays within that month. We usually have ice-cream cake (takes the place of having cake and ice cream separately) that simply says Happy November Birthdays. This way, no one is forgotten, and everyone looks forward to the meetings a little bit more, knowing that ice-cream cake is going to be served."

potential it has to create animosity between peers." Reinforcement, Keller pointed out, is not to be confused with incentives, which often are successful when they take the form of tangible rewards.

- Unpredictable. Genuine reinforcement is usually spontaneous, as it is delivered only in response to a good idea or action. Scheduled compliments, such as praise at the close of each meeting, seem phony and often have the opposite effect they were intended to produce.

"It's far more difficult to keep a team going than to start a team," Keller said. But if you practice peer reinforcement (and keep it sincere), you're one step closer to ensuring the continued success of your team and its efforts.

BOOST TEAMWORK WITH REWARDS

To promote team spirit and workplace relations, be quick to recognize coworkers for their achievements. This becomes especially important if you aspire to be a manager. Leaders who don't know how to give credit soon find that people don't want to work for them. But verbal praise isn't always enough.

Keep an eye out for these kinds of achievements:

- On-the-job success. This includes reaching goals and objectives, generating good ideas, helping with a tough task, or going above and beyond the call of duty. It's one thing to be praised by a boss. But it's another if peers recognize accomplishments because they do the same kinds of tasks themselves.

- Small courtesies. Don't forget to recognize when coworkers consistently do little things that add to workplace teamwork such as offering to help coworkers, welcoming and volunteering to acclimate new employees, and taking and delivering accurate phone messages. Your acknowledgment could take the form of a personal note or card, a mention in an employee newsletter, a small plaque, a coffee mug, or a bunch of flowers. Use your creativity and tailor it to the individual. A little personal recognition can go a long way.

JOIN THE COMPLIMENT CLUB

Sincere compliments are a surefire way to build work harmony. Unfortunately, within many group structures, they are few and far between. Psychologist George Crane identified this problem while teaching a course in social psychology at Northwestern University in Chicago. Several students from small towns felt lonely and unwanted in such a huge city. The psychologist set out to help them with this assignment by giving

ACTION IDEA

Today, think of two coworkers whose achievements deserve recognition. Look beyond the obvious (promotions, successful job project completion) for something that may otherwise go unnoticed at work (an outside class that was successfully completed, an act of volunteerism in the community).

them a mission: "Each day, you are to pay an honest compliment to three different persons ... every day for 30 consecutive days," notes author Tom Logsdon in *Breaking Through* (Addison-Wesley).

Crane explained that the students didn't have to like the people whom they complimented. And, he stipulated that each "feel good" message have a narrow focus.

Shortly after the exercise began, one of the small-town students told Crane, "Our 'compliment club' has removed my terror and loneliness. It has altered my entire outlook on life."

Try organizing your own compliment club. Commit to giving one peer positive feedback daily. Make it specific, such as, "Steve, you were really able to get to the heart of that marketing problem at today's meeting. I admire your logic." This kind of compliment generally means more because it shows your insight into the situation.

TWO MOTIVATION IDEAS THAT WORK

- **Story Time.** At Kaset International, a service quality consulting and training company, teams meet weekly to discuss different professional and developmental books. One member summarizes one to three chapters of the current book, and a discussion follows about how principles can be applied to their team.

- **Where Did They Go?** You never know where you'll find the quality-control team at Leckers, an Ohio manufacturing company. The team leader surprises members of the team by holding regular meetings in a different location each week. "We've been in the production plant, the research lab, and even outside on the front lawn," reports a team member.

... AND TWO THAT DON'T

- **What? No Pumps?** When the male members of a Chicago-based telemarketing team fail to meet their sales quotas, department policy requires that they must wear a woman's dress for an entire work shift. "It's motivation by humiliation," says one disgruntled team member.

- **Write Up This Dumb Idea.** At a Western utilities company, a team leader publishes "The Dumb Idea of the Month." "He thinks it's funny, but it's just embarrassing," says a former team member.

OK, You're the Leader: Now What?

As a worker in the company publications department, Holly Austin realized that some interdepartmental hang-ups were throwing many brochures and pamphlets off schedule. When management formed a "production pipeline" team to straighten out the wrinkles, she was pleased — but surprised — to find herself named as the team leader. "I was shocked," she says, "then scared, but I looked at the assignment as a challenge."

Here are the steps Austin took to get off to a strong start, and they'll work for you, too, when you're asked to lead a work group or team:

- **Get to know the team.** "I had brief discussions with the members' supervisor or coworkers," Holly recalls. "I knew many of the team members, but I had not worked with them and wanted to learn their strengths and talents."

- **Communicate constantly.** In a multiple-deadline process, communication is crucial, but the same thinking applies to any team situation. All members needed to know the full spectrum of work in the pipeline, so Austin started a daily production list of projects and their statuses.

- **Set up regular meetings.** Face-to-face meetings are essential. With her team, Austin determined that two group meetings a week would be the best schedule. To establish a routine, meetings were always at the same time and place, were as short as possible, and had a clear purpose.

- **Set goals with the team.** "I let team members set priorities within the broad deadlines the company determined," explains Austin. "Since the specific plan was decided by the team, the group was more willing to work within it."

Austin's basic goal-setting steps: involve all team members; identify the problem clearly; discuss the "payoff" to the company, the team, and individual team members; define "success"; list necessary actions; and make a plan.

- **Build a network.** To succeed as a team leader, Austin knew she needed the help not only of her team but also that of many other people in the company. To get started, she reviewed the organizational chart, listed at least one person she knew in each department, and notified that person of her new position. She also asked each of those people who they knew in other departments who might help solve the production pipeline problem. Soon, she had a list of "experts" she could call on as needed.

- **Listen, listen, listen.** Austin was accustomed to accepting assignments from supervisors and listening mainly to get instructions. But as team leader, listening took on another dimension. "I made sure the team knew that their feedback and suggestions were important," she says. "If I noticed that some members were troubled in a meeting or might have something more to say, I took a few minutes to talk with them later."

- **Motivate, reward.** "I would start every day with a positive comment on recent projects," she explains. "And when the team completed a major publication, we'd celebrate."

Austin's plan worked. The team soon became a permanent part of the company.

Asked to Lead? Don't Sweat It

Serving as a team leader or as the top coordinator for a departmental project provides you a good time to demonstrate your skills at motivating others. If you aren't used to serving in this more formalized leadership role, don't despair. A simple four-step plan can help you guide your team to increased participation and productivity.

Here's the plan, offered by Fran Rees in *How to Lead Work Teams* (Pfeiffer).

1. Lead with a clear purpose.
2. Empower to participate.
3. Aim for consensus.
4. Direct the process.

She explains: "Paying attention to all four parts of the L.E.A.D. model provides the leadership that any team needs," Rees says. "Leading with a clear purpose meets the need for common goals.

"Empowering members to participate achieves the high level of interaction and involvement that group members need. Participation and consensus help maintain individual self-esteem and encourage open communication.

"Participation and consensus also help build mutual trust and achieve a healthy respect for differences among team members while providing an avenue for constructive conflict resolution. Leading with a clear purpose and directing the process ensure attention to both process and content." Purposeful leadership means you use goals to motivate teammates. They must be realistic and tied to organizational objectives.

Publish the goals, make them visible, and talk about them. If you don't, nobody will remember them. Put your goals on posters. Refer to them often. As you reach milestones, celebrate!

"Your next move is to empower people to participate in achieving those goals," Rees explains. "Even though the goals motivate the team, your teammates will become unmotivated if they can't participate in important decisions.

"Sometimes you will be tempted to offer your opinion. But remember that one of the best ways you can empower others to speak up is to listen without having the final word." And don't let your teammates rely on you for answers. Ask each team member what he or she thinks. You're not giving up leadership. You're empowering others to share it.

The third step is to strive for a consensus that works through conflicts to achieve commitment.

Finally, direct the process. Use all your group persuasion skills to bring forth the best efforts of your teammates.

L.E.A.D. the way!

'WHACK' YOUR TEAM

Obviously, you want to be a motivated member of your team whose contributions are innovative and frequent. After all, no one wants to be stuck in a rut! But, like many things in life, getting started is often the hardest part of a commitment to motivation.

But, never fear. Even if you can't think of one single idea to motivate yourself and your team, you can borrow one or two from Barbara Glanz. The author, speaker, and consultant is practically bursting with ideas for "getting the creative juices flowing" in the workplace. Based in Western Springs, Illinois, she's compiled 399 real-life, how-to examples in her book, *The Creative Communicator* (Irwin Professional Publishing). Glanz shared her ideas:

Q: How does "creative communication" improve motivation?

BG: Creative communication adds spirit to the workplace. For far too long, most business communication has been predictable — and boring! I try to show people how to rise above the dullness.

Q: How about an example?

BG: At Hydro-Electric, one of Scotland's electric utilities, employees are invited to "indulge in some healthy, satisfying bureaucracy bashing!" Every employee can nominate a policy, practice, or procedure that gets in the way of extraordinary customer service. This type of communication differentiates that company from others and builds positive interaction. And Commerce Bank, in Coral Gables, Florida, has the "Dazzle" program. A department chooses a person to be "motivator of the week." This person wears a hat for easy identification and is responsible for "pumping people up" when they run down.

Q: Your book says your goal is to 'whack' a reader's thinking. What does that mean?

BG: In *A Whack on the Side of the Head* (Warner Books), Roger von Oech says we are all bound up in "mental locks." We need something to whack our thinking to help us see in a new way.
One of my goals is to whack readers into finding creative ways to communicate, to get the creative juices flowing. I am frequently asked: "How can we get our team motivated?" My answer: Be creative in different ways that surprise, even stun.

ACTION IDEA

The next time you're in charge of a meeting, try this 'whack' from Barbara Glanz: Post dozens of inspirational and motivational quotes on flip charts and bulletin boards along the walls. Give them a few minutes to browse the messages while they sip their coffee. They'll begin the meeting more motivated and energized.

Q: What makes employees *lose* their motivation?

BG: In all the talk about quality, downsizing, and technology, we've forgotten the human being. Creative communication brings it back where it belongs — to one-to-one communication that treats people with respect as unique, living, breathing human beings.

So, if you or your coworkers are feeling stalemated at work and bored with your jobs, whack yourselves out of your sleepy haze with a motivational exercise or contest. Remember that you do have control over your attitude.

Don't Let Those Ideas Get Away

You don't have to be intellectual or highly educated to come up with good ideas. Creative people have certain traits that distinguish them, but those characteristics can be developed with determination and practice.

Your job becomes easier and you are more productive when you make certain that no good ideas ever escape you. Although there are many ways to spark creativity, here are some tips to get you fired up:

- **Be accessible.** Since ideas may come from anyone at any time, you must be available to receive them. If you get the reputation of being hard to reach or in a hurry too much of the time, you can be certain that others will not go out of their way to pass along their ideas.

- **Encourage creativity and innovation.** You may receive a lot of unworkable suggestions. But don't let that discourage you — or those helping you — from coming up with ideas. Learn to put aside the unworkable ones graciously and tactfully so you don't turn off your coworkers.

- **Include everyone as a source for ideas.** Even reticent and introverted coworkers may offer good ideas. You might have to be patient and nurturing with them. But when these people eventually do respond, their offerings can more than make up for all of the waiting.

- **Study each idea carefully.** Take your time and avoid making snap judgments. Quick decisions are too often based on overall assumptions and intuition, and seldom on detailed analysis. Sometimes terrific ideas are prematurely rejected simply because time wasn't taken to thoroughly check them out.

- **Keep an open mind.** Since big ideas have a habit of growing out of little ones, avoid any tendency to pass by something minor. It pays to be alert for ideas that are not usable on the spot. With modification, they might be usable somewhere else.

- **Look into details.** Maybe a small error was made in the development and presentation of the idea. When that is corrected, the idea may be usable. Closer examination might even reveal that you can use one aspect of an idea for solving an entirely different problem.

- **File "bad" ideas and suggestions.** Today's impractical and unworkable procedure may be just the answer you need tomorrow. It's hard to remember every idea that comes your way. Months and even years may follow between an ideal presentation and the development of a situation where it can be put to use. Remember to always keep your notes on file, too. You never know when you might need them again. Why reinvent the wheel?

- **Never discount improvement.** Almost any process or procedure can be improved. If you decide something is perfect as is, you block out the possibility of considering areas for improvement. This provides a false and potentially dangerous sense of security.

- **Attack improvement hurdles and roadblocks from all angles.** Unusual procedures often can solve your most perplexing problems. Always turn a problem upside down in your search for solutions. Remember that good ideas can come from areas where you least expect them. Some of the best ideas ever developed were sparked by investigating an unfamiliar area of a business.

EXPLORE 'TEACHABLE MOMENTS'

An experienced shipping clerk shows a newly hired worker how to store packing material so it's readily accessible the next time it's used. A senior staffer shows a "junior" one a technique to check a payment voucher for errors before sending it to the accounting department. The resident computer whiz takes time to show a seasoned coworker a few shortcuts in a software program.

Every day, in businesses of all kinds, experienced employees provide one of the most effective forms of instruction outside of formal training. This instruction takes place in "teachable moments" — short periods of on-the-spot training. They're spontaneous, yet effective. Teachable moments do a great deal to increase efficiency, productivity, and team spirit, and the new knowledge can be applied immediately. Such ad hoc mentorship provides productive opportunities for experienced workers to share their skills and expertise.

Generally, as less experienced employees become more skilled, they, too, will follow their mentors' lead by showing others what they know. There are few other instructional practices that foster so much cooperation and teamwork.

Best of all, teachable moments require only a few minutes because they focus on a single skill. Feedback is immediate because of the opportunity to ask and answer questions. Retention is increased because information is presented in small, manageable amounts.

When you're presented with a teachable moment, consider these points:

- Identify the need. Keep your eyes open to observe where instruction is (or might be) needed. It's up to you to initiate the teachable moment.

- Justify the training. Identify the desired outcome. For example, you might stress that time is saved, productivity is increased, or frustration is minimized.

- Demonstrate and explain. Yes, it's critical to explain the *how* of a procedure, but it's equally important to explain the *why* to ensure understanding and maximize retention by the learner.

- Ask specific questions. This is the only way you can be sure your protégé grasps what you're teaching. Likewise, make yourself approachable so your student will feel free to ask any questions he or she might have.

- Perform a trial run. Seeing and hearing about a technique or procedure is one thing; actually doing it is another. Let the person get some hands-on experience, while you can observe (and correct if necessary).

It takes a minimum of time and effort on your part to have a productive teachable moment. And the rewards can be great for you, the learner, and the organization. Just consider what you accomplish by taking the initiative to help an unsure novice. Few, if any, of us are so busy that we can't spare a minute to help a colleague in such a profitable way.

CAREFULLY CRAFTING CRITICISM MAKES IT EASIER TO SWALLOW

One of the most important parts of being a team player involves letting others know when their actions and ideas are good ones — and telling them tactfully and constructively when they're not, says Jim Lundy, author of *T.E.A.M.S: Together Each Achieves More Success* (Dartnell).

The key to this kind of communication is to direct your comments at the behavior exhibited or concept presented by your teammate rather than at the teammate directly. "Focusing on behavior and actions, rather than traits, can make feedback more acceptable," says Lundy. "It leaves the recipient believing that change is possible."

If your feedback is critical, preface it with a positive statement: "I think you're on the right track with that cost-cutting proposal, and it could be even better if ... . " Notice that the word *and* is used rather than *but* to separate the compliment from the criticism. The word *but* often negates anything said before it.

PAIR UP FOR SUCCESS

Aldina Fuentes was frustrated. Each month, as production coordinator for a financial printer headquartered in suburban Chicago, she was responsible for tracking scores of pamphlets and brochures. Lately, the accounting department kept changing its paperwork procedures weekly. As a result, Fuentes often had to prepare a new report form, after being told that the one she had used last week was no longer acceptable. "Virtually nothing at work was routine anymore," she fretted.

Rather than grumble about the accounting department, Fuentes asked her boss if she and her coworkers could take advantage of a new company teamwork tool called pairing. In this organization, a pairing project is a way to bring together workers or departments, so they can come up with mutual solutions for any difficulties between them.

Fuentes related her frustration with the constant change in procedures. The accounting staff listened, then gave their reasons for the changes. As it turned out, the accounting department was shifting to a computerized financial tracking system and was testing various software programs. The result? Confusion.

The one-hour pairing meeting ended with an increased understanding on both sides. Accounting agreed to announce any changes as early as possible. Production has agreed to be more tolerant of the changes since they understood that the situation would be short term and benefit the company's bottom line.

In short, pairing is a low-risk, low-cost way to enhance teamwork and efficiency within an organization. It doesn't require special equipment or a big budget. And it generally produces the kind of communication needed for any company to perform at its best. Here are pairing-project basics:

- A facilitator. This is usually another staff member, but one who has no connection with either party and no vested interest in the issue. The facilitator's job is to keep discussion moving and guide it in a positive direction.

- Neutral territory. A conference room, small auditorium, or even a small office can be suitable, as long as it provides a degree of privacy.

- Positive attitudes. Healthy skepticism is helpful, but participants should not enter into a pairing session predisposed to failure or personal victory. Pairings exist to inform and explain, as well as to search for solutions. Most times, misunderstandings or problems are not any single person's fault. More often, problems are caused by flawed procedures or systems.

- Follow up, as needed. In Fuentes' case, she invited accountants to take a tour of her work area. During that friendly, informal visit, she was able give them a better idea of her situation.

ACTION IDEA

A pairing need not be so formalized or group-focused as the one above. Are you experiencing misunderstandings with a person in another department crucial to what your area does? Maybe a short pairing session with a neutral third party would help. You might be surprised how this information-sharing method can help you work better and build more productive work relationships.

DO COLLEAGUES FOLLOW YOUR LEAD?

Have you ever wanted to work for one of those organizations listed as "The 100 Best Companies to Work for in America"? Who wouldn't, and for good reason. Typically, these companies share certain characteristics. First, they offer employees stability and a steady pattern of growth and development. Second, they offer employees consistency. Employees are certain they will be treated equally under defined policies. Third, these companies offer flexibility in an environment that offers programs to meet the needs of staffers and their families.

What's the result? In general, these companies nurture a workforce that is enthusiastic, motivated, and committed.

One thing that doesn't appear on the list is a fourth characteristic. Model employers have model employees. Model employees help to transform an organization with their energy, dedication, and enthusiasm. A model employee is one whose work is more than satisfactory — it is exceptional.

How do you become a model employee? In most cases, model employees reflect the same values as their model employers. How do you rate in the following areas?

- Stability. Do you want to work in an organization that offers steady employment and chances for advancement? If so, you need steady work habits on which your employer can depend.

  Do you come into work a few minutes early to look over your workload and prioritize your day, or do you dash in right at starting time (or maybe a little later) each day? Are you willing to work through a regularly scheduled break or stay a little while after work to resolve a problem or meet the needs of a customer?

  Excelling in small things, such as punctuality and dependability, sets a good example for the rest of your office.

- Consistency. Do you perform brilliantly on occasion, yet turn in routine work that contains mistakes? Are you subject to mood swings, or can you turn the same smiling face to the public, even if you're feeling tired, anxious, or frustrated? Most managers don't like surprises from their employees, especially when it comes to performance. At evaluation time, you'll find that the consistent worker outperforms the brilliant, yet erratic, employee.

- Flexibility. Are you willing and eager to try out new technology, develop new procedures, or take on new assignments? Are you willing to take a leading role in developing an office team with spirit?

  In today's global marketplace, it's important to be flexible about the work you do because your routine could radically change tomorrow. Flexible employees don't fear change. They welcome the challenge. They constantly evaluate their own performance to produce the best work possible for today and tomorrow.

If you want more responsibility, you must show you can handle the work you do now. If you are stable, consistent, and flexible, you'll grow and develop personally and professionally. Work seems exciting. You bring out the best in yourself. The example you set will serve you well, and provide an excellent model for your colleagues to follow.

QUICK TIPS

- **Measure the positives.** Carry an index card at work for five consecutive days. Make a tally on the left side for every time you offer a criticism and a tally on the right for every time you offer positive reinforcement. To be an effective communicator, your positives should outnumber negatives 4-to-1.

- **Encourage introverts.** Enliven group discussions by encouraging people who don't normally speak up. For example, "Mary, I know you're knowledgeable about this issue. I'd sure like to hear what you think."

- **Get 'em talking.** To encourage a timid teammate to speak up, ask questions that require more than a simple "Yes" or "No" response: *Can you tell me about ...? How do you feel about ...?*

- **Give and get credit.** When summarizing discussions, recognize individual contributions by using names. Phrasing like, "As Wayne suggested . . . " or "Sue's idea was . . ." can go a long way to help people feel good about themselves, their work, and you.

- **Tell the boss.** When a colleague does you a special favor, send a written thank-you note. Then send a copy of the note to his or her supervisor. Your helpful colleague will get credit and visibility where it could really count.

- **Begin with brag time.** Start meetings with a brag time. Ask coworkers to share recent accomplishments that they feel excited about. This is a positive way to get people to think creatively as well as to give them their time in the spotlight.

QUIZ

Lead the Way in Creativity

"Lately I've become aware of how important it is to find creative solutions to problems. By reading a few books on the subject and talking with my mentor, I'm learning to make decisions more creatively. Now I'd like to encourage creativity in my teammates. How can I do this without causing offense?"
— *M.I., Boston, Massachusetts*

Without even mentioning the "c" word, you can encourage creativity by example. When you approach everyday problems and concerns creatively, your more perceptive teammates will likely notice and follow suit. To learn more about encouraging their creativity, take the following quiz. Answer each question with a YES or NO:

	YES	NO
1. Do you let others identify problems rather than jumping in too quickly with your own views?	___	___
2. Do you encourage people to challenge the way things have always been done in the past?	___	___
3. Do you support the free flow of ideas rather than cut off the brainstorming too soon?	___	___
4. Are you willing to entertain "far out" solutions as a way of breaking free of established thinking patterns?	___	___
5. Do you listen without judging when others are expressing ideas?	___	___
6. Do you tolerate ambiguity, accepting that often there are no "right" or "wrong" answers, only differing perspectives?	___	___
7. Are you flexible enough to change your mind when the evidence strongly supports another viewpoint?	___	___
8. Do you avoid putting others' ideas down, even when you think those ideas are totally unworkable?	___	___
9. Do you good-naturedly accept consensus decisions even when you don't agree with them?	___	___
10. Are you willing to take a calculated risk even though you can't be sure how things will turn out?	___	___

TOTAL NUMBER OF YES ANSWERS_____

Do you nurture creativity? A score of at least nine YES answers indicates that your creative approach to your daily job is probably a good example. If you scored fewer than nine YES answers, you might want to reconsider what creativity support involves.

YOUR CAREER SURVIVAL TAKE-AWAY

The 6th simple thing you *must* do to keep your job today (*and* tomorrow)

Motivate Others to Give Their Best

Working with highly motivated and enthusiastic people makes the workplace more pleasurable. That alone is good reason to do all you can to bring out the best in your coworkers. Motivating others also benefits you professionally: your immediate supervisor judges you on how well you can bring out the best in others. Motivation is contagious; working with others who are charged with motivation will get your juices flowing as well. And you can never do *your* best without the support of a team who is also striving for excellence. For these reasons, you should make it a top priority to do what you can to help others do their best. Remember the words of the 19th century English statesman Benjamin Disraeli (1804–1881): "The greatest good you can do for another is not just to share your own riches, but to reveal to him his own."

WHAT YOU CAN DO

- **Get in the habit of noticing opportunities to praise coworkers.** Everyone enjoys being praised, but few people take the trouble to praise others. Be in the minority. Develop a system that helps you remember to stop and notice a praiseworthy effort, performance, or result. Be your coworkers' biggest fan.

- **As team leader, foster a climate of innovation.** In brainstorming sessions, encourage employees to share their wildest and craziest ideas. Encourage your group to take risks.

- **Ask for advice and help once in a while.** Let your coworkers know you value their opinion. Once in a while ask, "How would you handle this …?" or, "This customer call really had me stumped. I recall you mentioning at a meeting once how you handled just this kind of problem. It sounded good to me. Would you refresh my memory?"

- **Share what you know with others.** "Teachable moments" are short periods during the workday when one person takes the time to show a coworker how something is done. When you put this idea into practice and show a personal interest in your coworkers, you not only increase their training, but also improve their motivation.

- **Encourage coworkers to share their knowledge with you.** Let others know how much you value their knowledge and experience. Ask them to share teachable moments with you. Not only will you become a more informed worker, you will gain further information about your place in the organization. This improves all-around productivity. You'll also help your coworkers realize how important they are and how much you respect them and the contribution they make.

CHAPTER SEVEN

Simple Thing #7:
LET SELF-ASSESSMENT AND SELF-DISCOVERY CHART YOUR WAY TO *CAREER* SECURITY

"Ninety percent of the world's woe comes from people not knowing themselves, their abilities, their frailties, and even their real virtues. Most of us go almost all the way through life as complete strangers to ourselves."

— SYDNEY J. HARRIS (1917–1986), AMERICAN NEWSPAPER COLUMNIST

INTRODUCTION

The biggest obstacle to career survival can be summed up in one word: *complacency.*

The minute we stop growing, the world starts passing us by. The minute we are reluctant to explore new ideas, new options, new approaches, that's the minute that we've allowed ourselves to become obsolete.

Business trends come and go. New technologies emerge. Customer needs change. In business, the only true constant *is* change.

The sad truth is, no one can promise you job security today. That's a reality of the work world as we approach the 21st century. But there is a promise you can make to yourself. That is, a promise to do something every day to give yourself long-term *career* security.

Career security is a future you create for yourself. The goal of career security is to be less dependent on your current source of income — your employer — and *more* dependent on yourself and your ability to earn a living. Career security is a process. It doesn't happen once, or even every ten years. It happens on a daily basis. It is possible only when we are willing to be open to change and growth.

Career security means treating yourself as a business. Just as companies and industries reinvent themselves to meet changing needs, you must constantly reinvent yourself to meet their changing needs. You need to be flexible. You must look in the mirror each day and see yourself as others see you. And after you've honestly evaluated yourself, you must be willing to change.

A willingness to change and grow . . . that's what this chapter is all about. We've listed this as the seventh of the seven simple things you must do for your career because, really, all six other "things" point to the skills you will uncover in this chapter.

In the pages that follow, we'll provide some of the tools for evaluating your attitudes and skills; you'll discover how to listen to (and challenge) the negative self-talk that holds you back, and you'll discover how to unleash your personal motivation and reach new heights of personal development and productivity. In essence, you'll learn how to listen to the single best "career counselor" you know — *you*!

WHAT WOULD YOU DO?

EASE UP ON YOURSELF!

*L*ately, you've been very hard on yourself. You put yourself down for minor mistakes. You seem to look for ways to lower your self-esteem. How can you turn your attitude around?

Start the turnaround *now*. As long as you have negative expectations of yourself, you can be sure you'll live *down* to them! A few tips:

- **Listen for the negative messages you're sending yourself.** Catch yourself and stop them. If comments like "I can't do this" or "You idiot!" run through your head, delete them immediately.

- **Sit down and make a list of the negative concepts you have about yourself.** For example: "I'm a bumbler" or "I never do well on tests." Replace those self-defeating concepts with encouragement. For example: "I'm competent, and I can do anything I set my mind to," and "I'm an intelligent decision maker."

- **Make a list of your strengths and successes.** Take out the list and read it whenever you start feeling down on yourself.

- **Accept the fact that you'll make mistakes.** Take responsibility for your errors, but don't beat yourself over the head when you don't live up to unrealistic standards. Remember perfection is a goal, not a destination.

CAREER PROGRESS DEMANDS TAKING RISKS

Moving ahead in any career usually requires taking risks. But risk frightens many of us. Fear is often a natural response to uncertainty, but you shouldn't allow it to limit your future or impede your progress. If your fear is holding back your career, here are guidelines that can help:

- Know what you want. Write down what you would like to accomplish professionally. For instance, you might want to suggest installing new software that is more user-friendly. Or you might want to toss your hat into the ring for that manager's position that will open up in February.

- Think about your goals, make them specific, and write them down. The act of writing will help you clarify your thoughts. Keep the document as a visible reminder of what you are working toward.

- Ask yourself: "What's the worst that can happen?" For people uneasy about taking risks, fear of the unknown is often much worse than reality. In truth, the boss is more receptive than they had anticipated, the proposal is given a fair hearing, or the interview for the new position is actually fun. To help you realize that the worst seldom happens, write down the most frightening outcome you can imagine. Just taking the time to describe your fear on paper can help lessen the anxiety.

- Identify the benefits. Now that you have considered what could possibly go wrong, take a look at what could go right. If you successfully take this risk, what benefits will you, your coworkers, the boss, and the company receive? For instance, perhaps you'll be able to cut a half hour each day off your time spent on correspondence, or you might be able to reduce expenses in the office.

- Write down obstacles. You can't leap into risk unprepared. Take time to consider possible outcomes. What challenges might you face? Do you anticipate disapproval? Will others question your authority or capability? Do you anticipate being embarrassed? How will you address possible objections? If you consider what might stand in your way, you can develop ways to overcome those objections.

- Visualize yourself taking the risk and succeeding. Create a mental picture of yourself talking to the boss. Imagine him or her expressing a concern, which you address confidently. Picture the boss giving you the OK. The more you can see your success in your mind's eye, the more likely you will be able to create it in reality. Think of your visualization as a "dress rehearsal."

- Just do it! Don't procrastinate by rationalizing that the timing's not right or that you need to be better trained or more prepared. If you find yourself floundering in these or other ways, review the benefits of your possible action and develop them.

Remember: the worst seldom happens. We create our opportunities. They are never tossed into our laps. Risk may cause some anxiety, but the outcome can be well worth the effort.

CULTIVATE YOUR POINTS OF POWER

Developing your leadership skills is essential to your own success, says Susan Woodring, director of learning at Blanchard Training & Development, Inc. in Escondido, California. Woodring identifies three key strategies for personal success:

1. Cultivate your "points of power." "Most of us tend to focus on our weaknesses," Woodring observes. "But when we focus on our strengths, we can really capitalize and build on them." Ask yourself, "Where do I have power or influence at work?" "You may have position power that comes with your title — division or team leader, for example," Woodring points out. "And you have task power when you're responsible for scheduling, say, or setting the agendas for team meetings." Consider also the power or influence you may have in these areas:

ACTION IDEA

Not much of a risk-taker? Talk to others with experience. Identify people who have taken risks and survived and progressed. These mentors can be a valuable source of information and inspiration.

Be prepared to learn from them; ask them detailed questions about their own progress. To what do they attribute their own success? How did they overcome their own doubts and fears?

a. Personal power. Are you articulate? A good communicator? Enthusiastic about your work? Do you have a good sense of humor?

b. Relationship power. Who is in your network who can help you or your team? Do you have a well-placed mentor, or someone who owes you a favor?

c. Knowledge power. Do you have certification or skill that gives you credibility? Cite these credentials to support your ideas.

2. Make sure you and your manager are "reading from the same page." Try this exercise: Write down what you consider your five key functions on the job. Then ask your boss or team leader to list what he or she thinks are your five key areas of responsibility. Both of you should also rank, in order of importance, the key functions identified on your respective lists.

Now compare the lists. Chances are there will be differences you'll need to discuss. "Studies show that you and your boss's choices are likely to match on only two out of the five items, so a dialogue can help you get on track," says Woodring. "Jobs and job descriptions are changing so rapidly these days that it's a good idea to do this exercise every three months or so."

3. Push problem solving. Do you come up with great solutions but find they don't get implemented? That's not unusual, Woodring says. "It's human nature to resist ideas that aren't our own." She recommends a strategy that will encourage others to accept your ideas: State the problem and its impact. Then come up with three possible solutions and point out the pros and cons of each to show you've done your homework. Now name your own choice and the reasons for your selection. Next, invite a response: "What do you think?"

By giving others a chance to make an informed choice, this strategy counteracts peoples' tendency to reject the ideas of others, says Woodring. It also shows them that you're a good problem solver, and it builds their confidence in your abilities. And it shows that you are someone who is willing to involve others in the decision-making process.

TIME TO CHECK CAREER GOALS?

"Even when opportunities are limited, you can set and work toward achieving your own career goals," says Stephanie Benjamin, president of Benjamin Associates in Doylestown, Pennsylvania. "We all need to take the time to think about what work we love doing," Benjamin says. "If you're not doing the work you really enjoy now, then try to find a way to start."

Begin by setting goals for your career growth. She recommends that you:

- Set broad goals. This first step helps you consider "the big picture" of what is possible. "'I want to learn how to be a marketing specialist' is a good example of a broad goal," Benjamin says. Set a deadline to reach your goal, she urges. Eventually, the broader goal will become more focused.

- Do a little research. Is this goal right for you? Benjamin's advice: "Go to the people who are already doing the type of work you're interested in. If you want to be a marketing specialist, for example, begin networking in the marketing department. Identify three people who may be able to help you. Tell them you're interested in marketing and want to know more about it. Then ask if you can work with them on a project or shadow them on the job for a day." Library research is also useful, Benjamin adds, because resources there give you organized information.

- Talk to your manager. "Schedule a meeting to talk about your goals," Benjamin advises. "But avoid the 'I'm really bored with my job' approach. Offer ideas to show that you want to take action — with guidance: 'I've been thinking lately about how I can grow professionally. I have a few ideas, and I'd really appreciate your input.'" Your manager may be able to provide opportunities for you to grow in the course of your current job, Benjamin points out. Perhaps you could be given more independence or authority or the opportunity to work on different projects in your own division or in coordination with other departments.

- Align your professional goals with company objectives. Ask for an informational interview with a key person in the marketing department, for example. You may discover that the company has a bold, new marketing project planned and is looking for highly motivated employees to take part.

- Identify resources and support. This could include a company workshop, a weekend course at a local community college, or funds for training. You also may need some form of support from your supervisor or team, such as a schedule adjustment or trading tasks with a coworker so you can attend a workshop.

- Acknowledge personal or corporate roadblocks. "You can deal with those roadblocks if you're aware that they exist," Benjamin stresses. "You may need to figure out how to raise the money for a marketing course, for instance, or how to convince a busy marketing specialist to give you 15 minutes of his or her time for an informational interview."

BECOME A LEADER IN CAREER AND IN LIFE

A large part of being a leader — in your career and in your life — is how well you know yourself and the people you work with. The United States Office of Personnel Management (OPM) has identified the intrapersonal and interpersonal skills necessary for attaining that leadership role. With nonmanagers assuming an ever-increasing share of the managerial burden, it is even more important for them to assess the extent to which they possess these skills.

Here's what you should know:

YOUR WORKPLACE, YOUR TEAM/YOURSELF. On his deathbed, Hubert Humphrey spoke about knowing one's own "irreducible essence." When all else is stripped away, what is it that defines you as a person? What defines your organization? What defines your relationships with your boss and your peers?

If we do not take time for occasional self — and organizational assessments, we run the risk of devoting our lives to things that ultimately have very little value to us. Look at how your job fits into "the big picture" of your life.

YOUR SKILLS. Review the following list of skills, established by OPM as a guide for career progression:

- Basic competencies: oral communication; leadership; flexibility; written communication; interpersonal skills; decisiveness; problem solving; self-direction; technical competence.

- First-level competencies: working with a diverse workforce; conflict management; team building; influencing negotiation; optimizing human resources.

- Mid-level competencies: creative thinking; planning and evaluation; client orientation; internal controls/integrity.

- Higher-level competencies: vision; external awareness.

As you go through this list, you should evaluate your competency in these areas and plan your path for improvement. Seek feedback from others about your progress.

YOUR GROWTH PLAN. Your growth will be closely tied to how successfully you work with your boss. But your estimation of your abilities in relation to your job requirements may or may not resemble your manager's perception. And if the two of you aren't working from the same foundation, your growth will suffer.

Ask yourself the following questions in evaluating the relationship between your job and your boss's job:

> What are your job duties?
> What does your job require?
> What changes does the future hold for your job?
> What obstacles are in the way of your performance?

Now, get together with your boss and have her answer these same questions about your job (for example, what does the boss think your duties, requirements, etc. are?). Once you compare answers, your goals and expectations will be better aligned with the boss's.

Your assessment of yourself, your company, your skills, and your growth is an ongoing process. Come back to it again and again as you work to become the leader you know you can be.

WHEN YOU WANT TO BE A LEADER

So you want to be a leader? All you have to do is act like one. What does that mean? You must be perceived by others as having the strengths and abilities required of a leader. But image will only carry you so far. You must prove, by your actions, that you really do have "the right stuff." Here are a few useful tips:

- **Identify role models.** Which individuals do you most admire for their leadership skills? What characteristics and qualities make you think these people are terrific leaders?

- **Meet with one of these team leaders.** People are nearly always willing to help and to talk about their own success. Explain that you would like to discuss leadership and will be asking for suggestions on how you can develop the necessary skills and abilities. Prepare a list of questions before the meeting and take time to think about them. Successful leaders know the value of being prepared. They don't waste other people's time — and don't like their time to be wasted either.

- **Study other leaders for their weaknesses.** What is it about them that turns people off? Perhaps they overstate their case, for example, or don't listen well.

- **Be a problem solver.** Leaders don't ignore problems, hoping they'll go away or somehow solve themselves. Instead, leaders are forward-thinking and solve potential problems before they can develop into crises. Leaders are also adept at involving others in problem solving, knowing that imposing a solution is rarely effective in the long run. They encourage input from others who are directly involved in the issue and then work for consensus.

- **Increase your visibility.** Start speaking up. If you're not comfortable talking to a group, take a public speaking course. You'll gain confidence and learn how to present your ideas in a compelling way that will interest and convince your listeners.

- **Try to get along with everyone.** The most effective leaders accept people's weaknesses and foibles and get the most out of people by capitalizing on their strengths.

- **Always be willing to lend a hand.** When someone's working on a tight deadline or is obviously overloaded with work, don't breathe a sigh of relief that it's not your problem. Pitch in. When you help one member of your group, you make a contribution to the entire team's success. And the team's success is the primary focus of every effective leader.

PLAN YOUR NETWORKING STRATEGY

The best professional networks don't happen spontaneously. They're built up over time with foresight and careful planning, says consultant Carole Hyatt.

First, Hyatt says, you need to set networking goals. Which people would you like to meet and why? You may want to explore certain issues, gain exposure to new ideas, and/or make connections that could be of value to you at work.

To achieve those goals, you need a plan. How will you make connections, or get the information or assistance you want? Smart networkers attend industry and professional meetings and conventions, Hyatt says. They review the agendas in advance and choose key people they want to meet. But you'll need a reason for introducing yourself at such events. Hyatt's advice is to create an "opening" for your introduction. Perhaps you've attended a previous talk or presentation given by the individual. You can mention that as you introduce yourself. If the person you want to meet has written a book, read it. "Then find something good to say about it," Hyatt recommends. "Flattery must be sincere, or it won't be taken seriously." Have compliments or appropriate comments ready when you meet the author.

Here are more networking pointers from Hyatt:

- **Let the individual know how to help you.** Be very specific: "I've recently taken on some leadership responsibilities for our team. I read your article about team players, and I was wondering what you feel is the most important trait of a leader."

- **Show your willingness to reciprocate.** "Networking is very much about give-and-take," Hyatt emphasizes. You might even launch the networking relationship with an offer of help: "At Green Co., we're implementing a new employee suggestion system. We've done a lot of research on this, and, if you're interested, I could send you what I have."

- **Don't bad-mouth others.** "The world is just too small," she says, "to get a reputation as someone who's untrustworthy, unethical, or difficult to work with. This network is your business and career safety net. In putting others down, you risk creating a gaping hole in that net."

ACTION IDEA

Think of it: If you know 50 people, and they each know 50 people, you have a potential network of 2,500 people! Before you can begin to tap into this huge resource, make sure you know exactly who is in your network and how you can maximize your relationship. Take out a pen and list all your contacts. Your list might include:

- *People at work*
- *Colleagues from previous jobs*
- *Customers*
- *Suppliers*
- *Friends in civic and community organizations*
- *Neighbors*
- *Relatives*

Once you've compiled your list, determine which of these people can help you achieve your career goals. What kind of contact from you would set the wheels in motion? Then list specific actions you can take to reach your prime candidates. Your list might include: "Join a civic group." "Schedule lunches with old friends." "Become more active in my trade or professional association." Then get started!

- **Expand your network.** Join at least three professional, business, and/or industry associations. "Take an active role in these groups," Hyatt urges.

- **Nurture your network.** Business relationships, like personal ones, require time, effort, and regular communication in order to thrive.

Your network can nurture you and your career for years — if you take care of it. Send thank-you notes when someone helps you. Send copies of newspaper articles you think might interest others. And, when appropriate, keep them up-to-date on what's happening with you and your career.

Train Yourself and Build Your Career

Take charge of your own continuing education, advises Kelly Tyler of Raytown, Missouri, a trainer with the American Management Association. Look for routine ways to improve your performance and image, and hone certain skills. For example, you can:

1. Develop a great memory. Use a mental pegboard. "Your mind can serve as a pegboard for keeping track of related information," Tyler explains. "Visualize a list of all your company's products in one section, for example, and telephone numbers of key people in another." Use association to remember names. For example, the Bob Jones you were introduced to today may have blond hair just like your friend Mary Jones back in grade school.

2. Be more flexible and open-minded. You'll appear more confident and competent if you don't insist on your own ideas and point of view to the exclusion of those of other people.

3. Think solutions, not problems. "If you're consulting with your boss about a problem that's come up," advises Tyler, "don't go in with, 'This went wrong — what are we going to do about it?' Instead, focus on solutions: 'Here are some ideas I have for fixing the problem.' "

4. Be a dependable source of information. "You project reliability when you always have useful facts and figures at your fingertips," Tyler points out. You don't have to keep it all in your head, she emphasizes. Her tips for being an information source:

a. Be a pack rat. Keep lots of information — such as reports, routine memos, and newspaper or magazine articles — that other people might be tempted to toss or file and forget.

b. Be organized so you can easily find what you want.

c. Know people at all levels of the organization. Draw on them as sources of information about their departments or areas of expertise. Be prepared to be a source yourself in return.

d. Tap the informal grapevine. "Pay attention to what people are saying," Tyler advocates. However, don't pass on gossip or unsubstantiated information.

5. Be someone who gets things done. Meet your project deadlines — and, even better, complete assignments before they're due. Help others with their work whenever possible, Tyler recommends, and graciously accept their offers of assistance. "Take on tasks that no one else seems to want to do," she urges. "People who are willing to go the extra mile are extremely valuable to an organization."

6. Avoid time wasters. "If your desk is in a high-traffic area, angle it so that you're not forced to make eye contact and talk with everyone who passes by," advises Tyler. "If people stop to chat when you're trying to work, change the subject by asking a business-related question or make an excuse to leave your desk to handle some task elsewhere." Always watch your time and be as efficient as possible.

BUILDING THE CREATIVITY HABIT DAY BY DAY

It's surprising how many people are convinced they aren't creative. But creativity is a learnable skill, not an inherited trait. And, once you learn this skill, it can be very useful on the job," says Evelyn K. Rice, corporate consultant with Rice, von Clemm Associates Inc, Greensboro, North Carolina.

"Using the skills of creativity can help you make the most of your talents, develop your self-confidence, and increase your level of self-motivation," Rice explains. "You'll get more enjoyment out of your job, become a more valuable employee, and gain an increased sense of control and mastery over your personal and professional lives."

Rice offers these tips for developing your creativity:

- **Free up your thinking.** Recognize that there are many ways to look at a problem — and many possible solutions. Thinking in terms of "right" and "wrong" solutions, and looking for that "one right answer," will severely curtail your creative exploits.

- **Overcome fear of failure.** The point of creative effort is to generate a multitude of ideas, so face facts now: You're going to come up with lots of unworkable ideas along with the good ones.

- **Think like an explorer.** "The idea-generating stage of creativity is a form of exploration," Rice points out. When you let your mind go exploring, you'll find yourself coming up with more unique and exciting ideas than you ever anticipated.

- **Schedule a creativity session to generate ideas.** Whether on your own or with your teammates, Rice advises, limit the idea-generating session to about seven minutes. This will ensure you won't get tired or lose your enthusiasm. Write down all of the ideas you come up with during this session.

ACTION IDEA

Start making a habit out of creativity.

• Start an idea journal. When the ideas aren't flowing, many writers put their random thoughts on paper. The writing isn't in any finalized form; the entries aren't for anyone else to see. But the journal may provide a spark when the writer needs his or her creative juices lubricated.

• Set creativity goals. Thomas Edison knew the importance of setting very specific and regular goals for his creativity. He was committed to coming up with a minor invention every three weeks and a major invention every six weeks. This was his way of developing his creative abilities and staying open to new ideas.

- **Don't censor yourself.** Don't evaluate your ideas as you generate them. "You want all of those wild and crazy ideas to come out," Rice notes. "It's easy to tone them down once you're ready to evaluate and decide what works best."

- **Have fun!** Get goofy. See how wild your ideas can get or who can come up with the most outlandish thought.

  "Humor breeds new ways of seeing and doing things," Rice says. "We've all noticed how creative children can be when they're just playing around, having fun. Interesting things happen when adults take a childlike approach to problem solving."

- **Write down ideas that just pop into your mind.** This tactic will encourage you to be creative spontaneously, without the "prompting" of a scheduled creativity session. Soon, you will automatically be asking, "How can we do this differently?"

EVERYONE VALUES SELF-MOTIVATED EMPLOYEES

Self-motivators are highly valued in today's rapidly changing business environment. They're creative and flexible, show initiative, and capable of maintaining a consistently high level of performance with a minimum amount of supervision.

To assess your own level of self-motivation, consider to what degree you have developed the following key characteristics:

- You're a self-starter who gets going on a project without being prodded or waiting for another's lead. It's easier to get underway on your own if you fully understand what is expected of you. When you're first given an assignment, ask as many questions as necessary. For example: What is the goal of the project? What part is to be completed first?

- You propose solutions instead of just complaining to your boss. If you focus only on problems, then you are part of the problem. Instead, become known as a problem solver. Take the time to consider possible solutions, and then be prepared to defend your idea with a plan for implementation.

- You take preventive action on potential problems. If experience alerts you that a certain problem is likely to recur, speak up before the situation reaches crisis proportions.

- You consistently meet deadlines. Deadline pressures are most likely to overwhelm you if you leave too much of the work involved in a project until the last minute. Be realistic about the amount of time you will need to complete phases of the assignment. Then, set mini-deadlines.

- When faced with a new task, you see it as a challenge rather than a problem. If you consistently find "the new" challenging, you show that you're willing to push yourself beyond your comfort zone to new levels of knowledge and competence.

- You speak up when you identify a need for improvement. You are, therefore, perceived as being in the forefront of change — someone who makes change happen rather than simply reacting to it when it's forced on you.

- You're willing to take risks. Sure, it can be scary to take a risk. But remember that even the most seasoned actors get the jitters every time they're about to step on the stage. So, don't let fear or doubt stop you from proposing solutions, presenting ideas, or expressing opinions. You may not convince people, but you'll be respected for "putting it on the line."

- You're committed to continually educating yourself, personally and professionally. Take advantage of formal training and other learning experiences provided by your organization. Read your daily newspaper to keep up with local, world, and business news. Scan periodicals related to your business and/or industry. Most importantly, always be willing to learn from others, regardless of their level within the organization.

Unwritten Success Secrets

Many corporate expectations do not appear in any handbook, according to *Executive Strategies*. People who find their careers at a standstill might consider these:

- Most promotions happen in sales and marketing. Why? Dynamic performance is easy to quantify. If you don't work in those areas, tie your ideas to sales and the bottom line.

- Look at your image. Do your fashions match top management's? If not, adapt your style to your company's, be it casual or formal.

- Follow social lead. If it's status quo to join the boss for socializing after work (and the movers and shakers do), join the club. Even if you drink tonic water and lime, this helps you get in step with fast-trackers.

- Cut down on vices. In today's workplace, employers frown on smoking and alcohol use.

- Inquire about other unofficial rules. Target friendly fast-trackers for some of their "trade secrets." Often, they are complimented by your inquiry because you think they are in the know.

Action Idea

If you discover you aren't particularly self-motivated, it's not too late to change. Start by naming one new idea you will propose to your team or your supervisor in the next few days:

_____
_____
_____
_____
_____

When you've completed the goal, review the outcome. How did your team react to your idea? Did it feel good for you simply to propose it (whether it was accepted or not)?

If you're comfortable with the outcome, push yourself a notch further. Set one more, slightly tougher goal. When it's completed, review your feelings again and take another step.

HERE'S HOW TO BE HIGHLY EEFFECTIVE

One of the most popular business self-help books on the market these days is *The Seven Habits of Highly Effective People* (Simon & Schuster) by Stephen R. Covey. But even the author admits that the habits he encourages are "nothing more than common sense." Still, he says, "what's common sense is not common practice."

Covey's seven habits boil down to how to become a secure and directed individual. As founder of the Covey Leadership Center in Provo, Utah, Covey is helping companies nationwide teach the seven habits to their employees.

Here are Covey's main principles:

- Be assertive. "You are the programmer of your life," Covey says. "Stop blaming others and start making things happen." Change your language and your thinking. Replace "There's nothing I can do" with "Let's look at our alternatives."

- Begin with the end in mind. How do you want to be remembered when you eventually leave your job? Use this as a vision for your daily behavior, he says.

- Put first things first. Instead of concentrating on what's urgent, focus on what's important. "We react to urgent matters," Covey says. "Important matters that are not urgent require more initiative."

- First understand, then be understood. "Most people do not listen with the intent to understand; they listen with the intent to reply,'" Covey says. "They're either speaking or preparing to speak." Be more effective by listening more and speaking less.

CREATE YOUR OWN HOPE TO CREATE YOUR OWN SUCCESS

"Hope springs eternal," goes the saying. Maybe that saying should be revised to: "Hope springs eternal for those who believe in hope."

Hope is, in fact, more than optimism, suggests C. Rick Snyders, a psychology professor at the University of Kansas. He defines hope as a pragmatic, goal-directed attitude that combines determination with ability.

What inspires hope? Snyders says:

- **Understanding that failures are not due to character flaws**
- **Remembering that each step toward a goal is a success in itself**
- **Constantly recalling past successes**
- **Viewing all people as potential allies**
- **Understanding that successful people aren't necessarily better — they simply have better coping strategies.**

JOB SATISFACTION TAKES PERSONAL EFFORT

You owe it to yourself to find satisfaction in your job. Work attitudes distinguish outstanding workers from mediocre ones. The mediocre workers lack self-motivation and the spirit to excel; the outstanding ones work with initiative, energy, and purpose. They feel a sense of accomplishment and are happy about themselves and their jobs. Their satisfaction and pride with the job and company don't make them complacent. They never stop feeling the urge to improve themselves.

Everyone has the potential to be either mediocre or outstanding workers. The mediocre self says, "I know I am not as good as the others. I can't do it." But the outstanding self says, "I'll make it. I know I can do it."

Lapses in self-esteem can happen to anyone. If this happens to you, realize that personal satisfaction comes from a mental attitude — the one thing you can control. Here are some tips that may help you to develop a sense of pride and personal satisfaction:

- Set realistic goals. Some people are frustrated and ruined by their unrealistic expectations. Realize that if you set an attainable goal within a reasonable time frame, you are apt to work toward the goal and achieve it. However, don't set your sights so low that you limit your potential.

- Prepare a list of positive personal traits. On a regular basis, compile a list of personality traits that you're proud of — your sense of humor, generosity, trustworthiness, and diligence. You might find that overall you are a terrific person whom you like. No doubt others do, too.

- Prepare a list of professional skills and special abilities. Include in this list your technical and professional skills. Seek your coworkers' advice if you are uncertain about them. You might be surprised to see how much expertise you possess.

- Don't expect to be perfect. You guarantee disappointment and defeat. If you find things about yourself that require improvement, don't let them spoil your day. Instead, take positive steps to self-improvement. Take a class you've put off, or do some homework on a subject in your spare time. If you take steps to ensure your personal and professional satisfaction, the workplace will be brighter. And you'll serve as an inspiration to others, too.

VIEW SUCCESS AS A STARTING POINT

Your latest performance evaluation was excellent, you've recently achieved several of your professional objectives, and you enjoy the esteem of your boss and peers. This can be a dangerous time for your career. "When you reach this level of achievement, it's important to enjoy your success and to take full credit for it. Unfortunately, this can also be a dangerous time if you become complacent with success," cautions Gerry Felski, productivity consultant and president of Integrated Learning Solutions in Merrimack, New Hampshire.

This is a time to reflect on your success. Self-evaluation can be very helpful in keeping you up to the mark and on track, ensuring future good work and success.

Felski suggests the following tips for self-evaluation during this period:

- Analyze the factors of your success to date. Take an inventory of your talents and skills. Look at other key factors that have worked in your favor, including your particular network of supporters. Consider how you can win the support of others who might contribute to your continued success.

- Pay attention to changes in the direction of your business and your industry. What new skills and knowledge should you start to acquire now? Plan how you can take advantage of company education programs, tuition reimbursement, apprenticeships, cross-training, and other future preparation opportunities.

- Read economy-related forecasts and trends in business publications. "These publications continually focus on where industries are going and where opportunity will be found," Felski says. "At the American Marketing Association meeting in Anaheim, California, in April 1994, it was projected that the majority of jobs to be found in the year 2010 have not even been created yet. Incredible opportunity awaits those who are prepared," he notes.

- Set professional "stretch" goals. "They force you to grow and stretch beyond your current skill levels, yet aren't so far out that they're unreachable," Felski explains. "Ask your manager to include your stretch goals as a separate category of self-development activities that clearly demonstrate your value and potential."

- Be aware of your need for fresh work challenges. "Sometimes, success isn't as satisfying as we expected it to be," Felski points out. "Instead of feeling great, we feel empty, restless, and/or bored."

If you're experiencing the downside of success, Felski suggests that you examine your personal and professional goals. You may have outgrown your responsibilities and need to pursue new chal-

ACTION IDEA

Keep an "accomplished" list. Many people keep a "to do" or "pending" list that reminds them of all the things they want to accomplish. At times, this can be discouraging if they don't accomplish all the things they intended to do.

Instead, keep a separate list of things that you have completed at the end of each workday. The list allows you to chart your progress, view yourself in a positive light, and helps maintain your high self-esteem. It's also helpful when you're due for a performance review.

lenges. "A lack of challenge doesn't contribute to success," Felski observes. "It's up to you to put yourself back behind the wheel and steer in a direction that will challenge and excite you."

REINVENT YOUR STORY OF FAILURE

Failure is no fun. It shakes our confidence. But we can recover pretty quickly by "reinventing" a story of failure into a tale with a more positive spin on events, says Carole Hyatt, co-author of *When Smart People Fail: Rebuilding Yourself for Success* (Penguin).

Here are Hyatt's guidelines for reinventing a story of failure:

1. Write a basic statement about what happened. Be brief and direct: "I lost the promotion," "My boss is unhappy with my work," or "The team I lead lost a contract."

2. Give your version of the event. You can write it down, record it, or tell someone you trust. Remember, you're giving your side of the story.

   Here's one example of a "personal story" for "The team I lead lost a contract": "Obviously, going out on a limb with new ideas doesn't pay off. I thought I had the support of the entire group, but, since we lost the contract, I feel I'm being blamed. The first thing they wanted to do was look at what went wrong. Well, I don't think that's going to help. Maybe what the team really needs is a new leader."

3. Look for the hidden message in your story. What negative and self-defeating assumptions are revealed? In the above statement, for example, we might "read" these messages as follows: "I'm a failure — I should be perfect," "Everyone else blames me for the failure," and "I don't have what it takes to be a leader."

4. Reinterpret your story in positive terms. Reinterpretation is a powerful tool for moving beyond an experience of failure. "If you tell your story as the tale of a loser," says Hyatt, "then you'll act like a victim. But retelling it in a positive way helps you act like someone who is in control."

   The teller of this story, for example, could view him- or herself as someone who is willing to take risks and who has the creativity to lead the team through both success and failure. He or she could also view the team's desire to "look at what went wrong" not as blaming and scapegoating, but as an attempt to take joint responsibility and learn from errors. Far from challenging his or her right to lead the team, the group could be looking to this individual to salvage something positive from their joint failure.

"Hidden patterns originating in childhood can color our perspective of and reaction to events in the present," notes Hyatt. We may have been judged harshly by a teacher or parent when our ideas failed, for example.

As adults at work, we may be very hard on ourselves when our risk taking doesn't have the desired results.

The bottom line: Look at everything you can learn from an event — and go on from there. That doesn't mean deny your experience of failure, Hyatt emphasizes. "Reinterpretation has its limits," she observes. "The basic fact remains: You did lose out on a promotion, or the team under your leadership lost the company a contract. But the way you interpret what happened is up to you."

GUESS WHAT? EXPERIENCE *ISN'T* ALWAYS THE BEST TEACHER

We take it for granted that we learn from experience. But is what we learn useful? Not when the lesson is to limit ourselves, according to *Florida CEO*.

Experience can be the "mother of convention" says Deanna Berg, Ed.D., of Innovative Strategies International in Atlanta. Relying on past experiences to choose a course of action *hurts* us when we:

• Let it limit us to repeating whatever worked for us before.

• Fear the unknown because our experience was negative or resulted in failure.

• Don't accept responsibility for our actions — especially when we make mistakes or fail in some way.

• Let what's happened in the past determine what we think is possible for the future.

• Stop trying to change because previous efforts to change have been unsuccessful.

The lesson here: Yes, experience is a helpful teacher — but only when it helps us grow.

NEUTRALIZE THAT NEGATIVE SELF-TALK NOW!

Negative self-talk is a destructive force based on misconceptions about ourselves rooted in childhood. "These misconceptions have such a powerful influence on our thinking and behavior as adults because they originate with the people we trusted the most," explains Sonia Ascher, of Ascher Associates, corporate trainers based in Nashua, New Hampshire. "I was told early that I couldn't carry a tune, and I believed firmly that I couldn't sing until very recent experience proved otherwise. But, up until then, my belief that I couldn't do it kept me from even trying."

Negative self-talk can take several forms, including:

• **Self-fulfilling prophecies.** "These are negative expectations we set up for ourselves," Ascher says. "Our self-talk goes like this: 'If I don't manage this project all by myself, they'll know I'm incompetent' or 'If I get up and speak at that meeting, I'll look like a fool.'

This is thinking in terms of absolutes — the never/always syndrome: 'I'll never be able to handle things' and 'I'll always be afraid to speak in public.'"

- **Going on "ought-o-matic."** We tell ourselves, "I ought to be able to get the top grade on this exam" or "I ought to do that for Joan even though I don't have the time right now."

"We put pressure on ourselves to be flawless," Ascher notes. "Our drive for approval makes us overachieve and not pay attention to our needs. Rather than look at ourselves through the eyes of others, we need to value how we feel about things. It's called validating yourself."

- **Placing blame.** We tell ourselves and others, "I am not responsible for my own actions." Says Ascher, "When we place blame, we look outside ourselves for reasons things don't work for us. We blame other people or the circumstances rather than accept responsibility." For example, "If John hadn't walked in late for the meeting, I wouldn't have been distracted and made a mess of my presentation."

Does negative self-talk interfere with your personal and professional relationships? Try these tips:

- **Track your self-talk.** Be aware of sending yourself negative or self-defeating messages. They begin with *I can't, I could never, I ought to, I should, I shouldn't, If I/he/she hadn't.*

- **Write down your self-talk.** Every time you say *I can't*, for example, write it down in a notebook.

- **When you're emotionally calm and objective, review the negative self-talk you've recorded.** Ask: "Why did I say that? Where did it come from? What happened in the past to make me believe I can't do X? What trusted person from my past am I really listening to when I say, 'I ought to,' 'I shouldn't,' or 'I'll never be able to?'"

- **Be objective.** Is your self-talk valid? Maybe it is, but maybe it isn't. Visualize yourself as you want to be.

"If you believe you can't speak well in public," says Ascher, "then imagine yourself confidently giving an intelligent and well-received presentation to your team." If you blame others when things go wrong, envision yourself standing tall and taking full responsibility. Then imagine the consequences: others supporting and respecting you for your honesty and accepting you with your imperfections.

BANISH THOSE NEGATIVE THOUGHTS

More than 200 negative thoughts a day. That's the norm for the average person, according to *Strictly Business* magazine. If you're depressed, you could average *600* negative thoughts a day. The good news is that you *can* reduce the number of negative thoughts you have, which include worries, anxieties, jealousies, insecurities, and cravings for forbidden things. Here's how:

- When you begin having a negative thought, stay quiet for a few seconds. Talking tends to intensify the negative feelings associated with that thought.

- Take five slow, deep breaths to lower your anxiety level.

- Visualize a relaxing scene such as walking on a beach at sunrise.

- Learn to banish negative thoughts. You'll eventually find that fewer of them surface.

QUICK TIPS

- **Look in the mirror and just say 'no.'** Know when to say no to yourself when trying to achieve personal goals. If you put too much pressure on yourself to achieve, you overcommit. What results are feelings of stress, guilt, and overall unhappiness. These overshadow any feeling of accomplishment you would enjoy otherwise.

- **Motivate yourself to think, think, and think again.** Follow IBM's lead: Before rushing to someone else when a problem arises, employees are expected to think about the problem three times before taking action. After the third time, they decide whether they can solve the problem on their own. If not, then it's okay to get help.

- **Make a statement.** Organizations, departments, and teams have mission statements, but what about you? Develop a personal mission statement for work. Ask yourself, "What is the unique purpose I fulfill at work?" Then, write down the answer.

- **Embrace the new.** Don't grouse about learning new things. View it as a challenge. How can it benefit your current work? How could it help you in the future?

- **Avoid getting in a rut.** Get in the habit of sitting in a different chair each time your department or team has a meeting. Most people are creatures of habit, but that kind of mindset can cause individuals to get stuck in ruts and miss varying perspectives. Rearranging yourself physically can help remind you to look at issues from different perspectives.

- **Be your own biggest fan.** Zig Ziglar, the motivational speaker, says a secret to personal success is to "work for progress, not perfection" and to "make your cause bigger than your ego."

QUIZ

Are You Moving Up or Down?

There are two ways to move in your career — up or down. Which direction do you want to go? The United States Office of Personnel Management offers the following list of skills as a guide for career progression, explains Dr. Marlene Caroselli, author of *The Language of Leadership*. Indicate on a scale of 1 to 5 (5 being the highest) your expertise in the areas listed below:

Basic Competencies

Oral communication	1	2	3	4	5
Leadership	1	2	3	4	5
Flexibility	1	2	3	4	5
Written communication	1	2	3	4	5
Interpersonal skills	1	2	3	4	5
Decisiveness	1	2	3	4	5
Problem solving	1	2	3	4	5
Self-direction	1	2	3	4	5
Technical competence	1	2	3	4	5

First-level Competencies

Working with a diverse workforce	1	2	3	4	5
Conflict management	1	2	3	4	5
Team building	1	2	3	4	5
Influencing negotiations	1	2	3	4	5
Motivating others	1	2	3	4	5

Mid-level Competencies

Creative thinking	1	2	3	4	5
Planning and evaluating	1	2	3	4	5
Understanding customer needs	1	2	3	4	5
Integrity	1	2	3	4	5

Higher-level Competencies

Vision	1	2	3	4	5
Understanding your competition	1	2	3	4	5

Your Total Score: _____

Which way are you moving? Below 50: Spend more time developing the skills you have and acquiring some new ones. 50 to 75: You need to refine rather than acquire. Heighten your awareness of what works and what doesn't. 76 to 100: You know what skills get you ahead, and you know how to use them. Now begin looking for ways you can positively influence your coworkers by example. You'll grow in the process.

YOUR CAREER SURVIVAL TAKE-AWAY

The 7th simple thing you *must* do to keep your job today (*and* tomorrow)

Let self-assessment and self-discovery chart your way to career security

Since your odds of having one employer for a lifetime are no longer very good, you have to look beyond mastering the particular skills you need to hold onto any one job. Instead, you need to think of long-term career security. That's the security you create for yourself. It is possible only through flexibility, an open mind, and a willingness to grow and change. Assessing your skills, attitudes, and motivations can help you find new areas of career advancement and new ways to direct your career. Networking puts you in contact with people who can help you reach career goals. Spending time with yourself — getting to understand your own motivations, your career and personal needs — will set you on a path that is personally satisfying. You'll create a new definition of job security for yourself — one that recognizes that security lies *not* in outside forces, like your employer, but in internal forces: your attitude, mindset, capabilities, and expertise.

WHAT YOU CAN DO

- **Make a commitment to constant learning.** Set a goal to learn one new job-related skill a month. Read industry journals to stay on top of the trends that affect your organization.

- **Let others see that you are self-motivated.** Employers like self-motivated people because they are creative and flexible, show initiative, and are capable of maintaining a consistently high level of performance with a minimum amount of supervision.

- **Learn your personal points of power.** What are your strengths? Build on them and capitalize on them to achieve your goals.

- **Get to know your colleagues.** Expand your network within your company by talking to people of all levels in departments other than your own. Learn what they do and inform them of your own job functions.

- **Catch yourself when you indulge in negative self-talk.** Make a conscious effort to change what you say to yourself from something negative to something positive.

PART II

THE CAREER SURVIVAL TOOL KIT

CHAPTER EIGHT

Career Survival Tool #1:
MANAGING STRESS:
KEEPING COOL & CALM UNDER PRESSURE

"Nothing gives one person so much advantage over another as to remain cool and unruffled under all circumstances."

— THOMAS JEFFERSON (1743–1826), 3RD PRESIDENT OF THE UNITED STATES

INTRODUCTION

You're busy. The work is piling up. The phones won't stop ringing, you've had to skip lunch, your stomach is in a knot, and the boss wants that report NOW.

You master the latest technology just as it is outdated. You have survived buyouts and takeovers, and now your company is downsizing. Again. So you are scrambling to do twice the work with half the resources and in a third of the time you once had.

Welcome to the workplace of the mid-90s, where Americans consistently rank their jobs as the number 1 source of stress in their lives. "People today equate work with stress," says Mitchell Marks, a psychologist and author of *From Turmoil to Triumph: New Life After Mergers and Downsizing* (Lexington Books). "Unpredictability is now the norm," he adds. "So get used to it."

As if you needed proof, a series of studies purport to show exactly how bad it is:

- U.S. wage earners log the equivalent of an extra month of time on the job compared with workers two decades ago, according to a study by Harvard University economist Juliet Schor, author of *The Overworked American* (Basic Books).

- Record numbers of people — upwards of half — say they'd be willing to take less pay for more free time. "The people who trade in comfort for more free time identified balance and less stress as their motivation," says Schor.

- The American Institute of Stress reports that as many as 90 percent of all visits to primary care physicians are stress-related, ranging from stomach trouble to heart disease. The institute estimates that job-related stress costs American business $150 billion a year.

- Sixty-one percent of respondents to a survey by the Families and Work Institute in Manhattan said that in the past three months they've felt emotionally drained; 75 percent said they felt used up at the end of the workday; and 70 percent reported feeling tired in the morning when they get up and face another day on the job.

"One of the results of downsizing is that people are having heavier workloads," says Deborah. K. Holmes, a senior research associate with the Institute. "Not surprisingly, workers with heavier workloads report more burnout."

To become truly indispensable, above all else you need to physically survive the pressures of the new working world. That's why we consider learning to manage stress as the number one tool you'll need in your Workplace Survival Tool Kit. In the following pages, explore the types of pressures you're facing on the job today and some of the strategies for coping.

WHAT WOULD YOU DO?

TAKE STEPS TO DEAL WITH BURNOUT

In the past few months, you seem to have lost all of your enthusiasm for a job you used to love. You find you don't even like to get up in the morning on workdays. You don't sleep well anymore, and you literally have to force yourself to go through the motions to get yourself to work on time.

You have all the symptoms of burnout. If you don't heed those symptoms and take steps to deal with your burnout, you could end up with even more serious physical and emotional problems. So, let's get started!

To start the healing process, acknowledge that you are, in fact, burned out. Admit it first to yourself. After that, depending on the program you follow and your working environment, you may well admit it to coworkers, supervisors, family, and friends. For most people, it's important to get support and encouragement from as many people as possible. You also can take comfort from knowing you are not alone: Employee burnout costs the United States more than $40 billion annually. Here are more steps you can take to heal burnout:

- Talk with your supervisor about employee-assistance programs. Be prepared to discuss your symptoms and the reasons why you think you've burned out. You may want to talk with someone from your human resources department first.

- Think about the most stressful aspects of your work and home life and how they could be contributing to your burnout. Just sit down with paper and pencil and list things you "hate to do." A tactful friend or spouse can also help by telling you which activities appear to upset you.

- Decide how you can eliminate or minimize key "stressors." For example, thoughtful consideration may show that you don't allow enough time to get to work in the morning. Getting up 15 minutes earlier could bring immediate, if temporary, relief.

- Consider all of your options. It may be possible to cut back on your workload, for example, or even move to another, less demanding division of the company that will offer you fresh challenges.

- View burnout as an opportunity for change. It is not a sign that you're a failure or that you can no longer handle your responsibilities. It's a warning signal that things are out of balance in your life.

- Learn from your experience. What permanent, if only minor, changes can you make to ensure that you don't reach a crisis point again? And take heart. A simple shift in attitude or perspective can help heal burnout and revive your enthusiasm for work and your joy for living.

ACTION IDEA

Think of one of the leading causes of your stress at work.

_____

_____

Next time you are face-to-face with that stressor, how will you react or respond to lessen the stress? (Responses might include delegating, allowing enough time to get tasks done, and saying no to commitments you just can't handle — without feeling guilty.)

_____

_____

_____

_____

STRESS SOURCES VARY FOR MEN AND WOMEN

Bosses, husbands, wives, the IRS, racism, office politics, and single parenthood are just a few of the stressors weighing people down today, according to a survey conducted by Dr. Donna Watson, a stress consultant and author of *101 Simple Ways To Be Good To Yourself* (Energy Press).

The respondents of the survey included men and women from all segments of society, from the unemployed and employed to homemakers, physicians, and attorneys. Each was asked to name the top stressor in his or her life. What's clear is that men and women differ in their perceptions of what they find stressful.

For men, the top 10 stressors included dealing with difficult or ineffective people; time management; overwork; negative attitudes; customers; finances; bosses; deadlines; balance; and performance evaluations. For women, the top stressors were time management; balance; conflict and communication problems; bosses; finances; difficult people; lack of support; coworkers; and negative attitudes.

"It's interesting to note that most people could not limit themselves to naming just one stressor," says Watson. "For most, stress is coming from multiple directions. I was also surprised that money and finances did not appear closer to the top of everyone's list, particularly given today's tough economic climate."

Other top stressors named by men were the economy; school; wives; lack of control; the IRS; reorganizations; meetings; communications; and weight control. For women, other stressors included family; overwork; perfectionism; layoffs; single parenthood; husbands; traffic; motherhood; eating; and racism.

It's important to remember that situations do not cause stress, adds Watson. It's how we *react* to situations. We can keep stress in check by knowing what our personal stressors are. Then, people should focus on responding to stressful situations, not reacting to them, she says. "For example, say you're cooking dinner for the family and burn a pot of potatoes. What would you do?" she asks. "If you start hollering at everyone, you're reacting to the situation, and your stress level skyrockets. But, if you take it in stride, move on, and try to calmly and rationally remedy the problem, you're responding and remain in control. As a result, your stress level drops."

Watson claims that we all should find small ways to treat ourselves well. This might include engaging in playtime, spending time with friends and family, or pursuing a hobby or leisure activity.

To survive in today's world, you have to be your own best friend, and that includes treating yourself in the best ways possible. Make a point to take better care of yourself, both physically and mentally.

TAKING CARE OF NO. 1

To perform your best, you need to feel your best. Here are a few tips to boost your physical and emotional health:

- **Take a breather.** For some people, getting away for frequent short breaks can be more beneficial than infrequent longer ones. Many hotels offer weekend packages for vacations near home. If you can't get away for an entire weekend, treat yourself to a movie, an evening of dinner and theater, or other special activities you enjoy.

- **Exercise.** A daily workout will give you a physical boost and help relieve the stress built up during the workday. Start small and gradually work up to longer sessions. Even walking can improve your health and your spirits. Consult a physician before tackling anything strenuous.

- **Get involved.** An interested person is an interesting person. Find something that you love, believe in, or care about. Then get involved. You'll benefit others and feel good about yourself, too.

- **Call a friend.** If you want help or company, you have to ask for it. Sometimes spending quiet quality time with a trusted friend can be a great buffer for workplace pressures and concerns. Don't forget to laugh.

- **Play.** We all need some fun in our lives. Figure out what makes you happy and then do it several times a week.

- **Just relax.** Schedule time for taking a long, soothing bath, reading a good book, meditating, or just daydreaming. Divorcing yourself from workplace stress can help you beat it.

SIMPLE STEPS BEAT STRESS

Stress is unavoidable in today's fast-paced world. But it can be controlled. Consider these tips:

- **Talk it out.** When something worries you, don't bottle it up.

- **Escape.** When things go wrong, it helps to get away from a problem, as long as you return later to solve it. Temporary distancing can boost objectivity.

- **Work off your anger.** Do something constructive with your pent-up energy. Play tennis or racquetball, do aerobics, or take a brisk walk.

- **Do something for someone else.** A good deed can take your mind off of yourself and make you feel good in the process.

- **Take one thing at a time.** Identify your most urgent tasks and focus on each one separately. Complete one before you move on to the next.

ACTION IDEA

Happiness is a choice, say Gary D. McKay, Ph.D. and Don Dinkmeyer, Ph.D., psychologists and coauthors of How You Feel Is Up To You (Impact Publishing). They suggest:

Today, write "Enjoy myself!" at the top of your to-do list. "This will remind you of what's really important in life," say McKay and Dinkmeyer. "Having joy doesn't mean you're shirking responsibility or being unrealistic. It does mean, however, that you're energetic and optimistic. And, those are two traits that are invaluable to your career and life in general."

ACTION IDEA

No one needs to tell you — you know you need more sleep! But how do you make time for the extra zzz's? Margo Baron, a Phoenix, Arizona, sleep researcher, suggests this:

• Go to bed 15 minutes earlier tonight. Maintain that schedule for one week. Don't change the time you're waking up. Don't sleep in on weekends.

• Next, add 15 more minutes for one week. Continue adding 15 minutes each week until you begin waking up feeling fresh and awake.

"Even though your body wants the additional sleep, you need to gradually condition your body to the changing pattern," says Baron. "Adding 15 minute increments helps because you need only make small adjustments to your waking hour schedule."

• **Shun the "superhuman" urge.** No one can be perfect in everything. Do your best, but be sure to forgive yourself quickly if you make an error.

NO SLEEP IS A NIGHTMARE ON THE JOB

Most Americans just don't get enough sleep, and that causes problems at work and on the road. That's the conclusion of a recent study sponsored by the National Commission on Sleep Disorders Research (NCSDR). "A substantial number of Americans are functionally handicapped by sleep deprivation on any given day," the report notes.

Today's cultural and economic forces have created a "24-hour society," according to the report, and millions of Americans, either chronically or intermittently, get insufficient sleep. The resulting sleep deprivation leads to inefficiency, lost productivity, and accidents.

University of Pennsylvania psychologist Dr. David Dinges has conducted tests which indicate that sleep deprivation reduces a person's ability to concentrate by 50 percent. That's one reason 60 percent of fatal single-car accidents occur between midnight and 6 a.m. Dinges calls this period the "fatigue hazard zone." Statistics cited in the NCSDR report indicate that, during the last century, Americans have reduced their average night's sleep by 20 percent.

How much sleep do we really need? The Commission says adults should sleep at least seven hours a night, but some people need more. About one in 100 people can get along on 5-1/2 hours of sleep (or less); 1 percent need 10 hours or more.

How can you tell if you've reached your optimum sleep quota? University of Florida sleep researcher Wilse Webb provides this common-sense measure: If you feel rested when you wake up, and don't get tired until bedtime, your sleep time is fine.

Sleep deprivation has far more serious consequences than just feeling tired, says health reporter Daniel Goleman, in *American Health* magazine. "Mental performance suffers," he notes. "Fatigue darkens mood and impairs concentration, memory, and decision-making ability."

Goleman also says that the longer a person skimps on sleep, the more the effects build up. People who are sleep deprived, he says, adapt to these changes and don't realize they're working at a diminished capacity. Here are some sleep tips offered by "wide-awake" experts:

• Are you chronically tired? See your physician. You might have a medical problem.

• Treat yourself to an extra hour or two of sleep at least one day a week.

• Keep a sleep diary. It might indicate that you need to forego (or videotape) that late-night talk show.

• Be wary of sleeping pills. Although helpful for occasional bouts of sleeplessness, they lose effectiveness after a week or so. Also, going off them too quickly can lead to withdrawal symptoms such as nightmares and nervousness.

- Be consistent. Go to bed and get up at the same times each day. If you are late to bed, get up at the regular time anyway.

- Drink milk. It's a good source of carbohydrates, which encourage the production of serotonin, a sleep regulator. The milk can be warm or cold.

If you've noticed that fatigue is cutting into your on-the-job effectiveness, don't ignore it. The condition may be serious, but the cure might be as simple as a good night's sleep.

EMPLOYEES REALLY ARE SICK

If you think most workers take one or two sick days when they're not really sick, think again. When asked: "In a typical year, how many days, if any, do you call in sick to work when you are not really sick?" 76 percent of the 671 adults surveyed, said, "Never."

The survey, sponsored by Accountants on Call, a temporary placement agency, also found that only one in seven of those who do call in sick when they really aren't, confess that they call in once or twice a year. Another 9 percent admit that they call in sick at least three times a year. Other survey findings:

- Employees under the age of 30 are most likely to call in sick when they are not.

- Part-time employees are more apt to take advantage of sick-day benefits.

- Employees living on the East Coast are more likely than those from other regions to call in sick when they are not (30 percent vs. 22 percent).

Becoming an "indispensable" employee does not mean never taking sick days. It means taking them when they are necessary.

DESKTOP STRESS STOPPERS

Just sitting at your desk can be hazardous to your health, according to *Stress-Free Living.* The way you sit in your chair, hold the telephone, or work at your computer can lead to repetitive strain injuries, says Christin Grant, Ph.D., a research associate with the University of Michigan's Center for Ergonomics.

But you can prevent or reduce muscle strain and soreness from repetitive movements on the job, says Grant. Here are her tips:

- Don't use your chin to hold the receiver against your shoulder when you talk on the telephone. The strain on your neck muscles each time you do this builds through the day.

- Sit up straight when working at your keyboard. Don't slouch or hunch over. Monitor and correct your posture regularly.

- Get up when you need to move around your office rather than staying seated in your swivel chair and using your legs to "walk" yourself around.

- Every 10 minutes take a 30-second break from tasks that require any type of repetitive movements. Change your body position, straighten your posture, stand up, roll your shoulders, and flex your neck or fingers. All of these movements relieve tense muscles and stimulate blood circulation.

- Take "R & R" on schedule. Don't make a habit of skipping coffee or lunch breaks in order to work straight through and get a job done faster. Your body, mind, and work will ultimately pay the price in pain, stress, and quality.

WORK IS JUST PART OF A BALANCED, FULFILLING LIFE

It's 9 p.m. You're still at your desk. You planned to get home on time, but the phone kept ringing. That unscheduled meeting ended up taking most of the afternoon. Then there was that last-minute package to get out. And you wanted to finish that memo . . .

Is this dedication or work addiction? Work-addicted people are driven by their own adrenaline. They actually create crises to stay out of touch with their feelings, says Linda Bryson, a Corvallis, Oregon, behavioral consultant. "Workaholics are in a constant state of fight or flight," she says. "They chase their own tigers, and the stress can result in health problems." In the end, their work can also suffer.

Bryson says adults who grew up in dysfunctional families are at particular risk of addictive behavior, whether the addiction is work, food, liquor, or something else. "Many workaholics were raised to be heroes of the family," she notes. "And they work to earn the praise they need to feel worthy."

What's the difference between those who are dedicated to their work and those who use it as a crutch? "Healthy workers feel a sense of purpose in what they do," Bryson says. "Work gives them joy and self-esteem. They experience stronger peer support and respect, and they function as a healthy team member with their coworkers." Work addicts, by contrast, tend to prefer to work alone. They hold perfectionist standards for themselves and others, and they get upset when those standards are not met. They are happiest when in control and like to do several things at once while racing against self-imposed deadlines.

"This frenzy of activity keeps workaholics from addressing unfinished business in their personal lives," says Bryson. "They may have grown up with a parent who was a controller and have never explored how that person made them feel." Ironically, these people often end up working for bosses with the same characteristics as the controlling parent. Some families even encourage work addiction by coveting material rewards the behavior can bring. "Other families may end up in divorce because the material and emotional needs are not being met," Bryson adds.

If you suspect you're addicted to work, Bryson suggests:

- Find a healthy support group or network. Join a 12-step program, such as Adult Children of Alcoholics and Dysfunctional Families. Or contact Workaholics Anonymous, P.O. Box 661501, Los Angeles, CA 90066 (310) 859-5804.

- Read books and attend workshops. There's a considerable body of literature on addictive behavior that can help you better understand it.

- Find mentors who live healthy lives. Meet with them regularly. They can help you learn how to attain goals without addictive behavior.

- Take care of yourself. Learn to relax without guilt. Get proper nutrition, rest, and exercise. Appreciate the present. Develop hobbies and commit time to socializing with family and friends.

- Seek professional help if needed. Change work behavior. Slow down. Learn to say "no" to extra tasks and projects. Build breathing room into daily schedules.

Those who buck addictive behavior may find it disquieting, Bryson says. What they think of as boredom may actually be serenity in disguise.

BREAKING MENTAL LOGJAMS

We are often our own biggest obstacle when it comes to problem solving. Our creative powers can remain reined in because we tend to define problems narrowly, to avoid looking foolish, and to cling to long-held beliefs through force of habit. These suggestions can help you overcome self-imposed limitations and unshackle your natural ingenuity:

- Fight fear of taking risks. Ask yourself what the worst possible consequences of an action could be. You'll realize that the world won't come to an end.

- Remember, you're smarter than you think! In high-pressure situations, people often surprise themselves with "newfound" abilities. Avoid such self-defeating beliefs as "I am no good at math." These negative perceptions will cause you to avoid math-related problems. Instead, face them head-on.

- Divide big problems into smaller ones. This way, you'll avoid being overwhelmed and defeated. Solve each part separately. When one is finished, move on to the next.

- Think in reverse. Start with the end of the process — the goal. Example: Consider how a truck will be unpacked at its destination and then move backward to determine the best way to load the truck.

ACTION IDEA

Write down one project that you've been postponing unnecessarily.

_____

_____

_____

_____

Choose one step of the project you can begin today (organizing materials, research, etc.)

_____

_____

_____

_____

Commit yourself in writing to a time you will begin this first step and the time you will stop working on it today:

I will begin the first phase of this project today at _____.

I will work on it at least until _____.

Make a written commitment each day until the work is completed.

- Don't "reinvent the wheel." Know what others in your situation have done and are doing. How? Ask a lot of questions.

- Put your ideas on paper. Conceptual devices, such as flowcharts and diagrams, can help you see the big picture, keep records of your thoughts, and find gaps in thinking.

TACKLING TOUGH JOBS LIFTS SPIRIT AND SELF-ESTEEM

It's inevitable. Sooner or later, you'll be assigned a project so incredibly boring, unpleasant, or difficult that it terrifies, upsets, or depresses you.

How's that for positive thinking? The task might be vital to the company or to your career, or it might be relatively minor in the grand scheme of things. Either way, you've got to do it — but you don't want to.

What's the best way to handle these tough jobs? Here are some guidelines:

- Act immediately. Start work today. Delay will only increase the unpleasantness. Postponement will introduce guilt or lead you to overinflate the task's difficulty. Your first step doesn't need to be major. But it should happen, even if it's just beginning a file, writing or reading the first page of a report, or plotting out the benchmarks on your calendar.

- Organize. Gather necessary materials or documents, create files, and set up required appointments. These activities also reinforce your action to get started.

- Identify the tough parts. It's important to know the points where the road gets rocky and invest time thinking about ways to overcome them. To keep momentum, complete at least one major part early. It usually doesn't pay to just nibble away at the edges of a big project — you eventually must take a big bite.

- Draw a finish line. There are few things worse than an open-ended schedule for difficult tasks because they don't get done. If the boss imposes a deadline, set your schedule to finish the project before that deadline. This allows some extra time for fine-tuning if you need it. And if the project gets completed early, you'll impress the boss.

- Be practical. Never turn projects into frantic rush jobs if they don't need to be. The idea isn't just to get the job done, but to get the job done well. Work at a comfortable pace that works to your advantage.

- Ask for help. Don't go it alone. Get advice from colleagues, friends, and supervisors. Ask for pointers from people who have done the job before. Often, just talking it out with someone can motivate you to tackle the job with vigor and enthusiasm.

- Take breaks. Once a project has been started, take occasional breaks to recharge your batteries. You don't have to suffer that much. Taking your mind off the task frees your imagination and might lead you to think of new approaches.

- Track progress. Give your boss informal, but frequent, progress reports. Keeping the boss informed keeps you on your toes and adds incentive for finishing the task. Celebrate at the halfway point. You deserve it.

- Finish and let it go. Once you've checked your work and it's completed, don't agonize over it or worry that it could have been done better. You've earned that feeling of relief and satisfaction that comes when a tough job has been finished. Enjoy it.

Once started, those tough projects don't seem so daunting. In fact, most difficult jobs are the ones you haven't started yet.

Oh, yes: When you finish, we guarantee you will be thinking positively.

SENDING OUT GOOD VIBES TO OTHERS

Your work space influences your level of stress and the attitude you project to coworkers and customers, and you can influence it by tapping into an ancient way of fostering good fortune, according to Nancilee Wydra, author of *Design Your Own Happiness: A Contemporary Look at Feng Shui* (Heian Books).

Pronounced "fung shway," the ancient Chinese discipline holds that environmental elements affect well-being and success. Wydra says plants, shells, or a fish tank can keep you in touch with nature. A mechanically moving, energy-enhancing object called a "chi" can also be a good influence.

Our advice: These ideas may help, but don't forget good old-fashioned courtesy and friendliness. We guarantee they'll send a positive message to customers and coworkers.

BOTTOM LINE — FUN

Who is that guy in the cancan dress? At Phelps County Bank in Rolla, Missouri, it might be one of the employees.

Phelps CEO Emma Lou Brent says workers' high level of commitment at Phelps had caused stress, reports Business Ethics. When bank employees stopped having fun, productivity declined. But, now, the bank allows time for fun. Recently, male employees danced the cancan, in appropriate costumes, at a staff meeting.

Brent credits the initiatives with helping the bank reduce overhead by 3 percent and increase net income by 32 percent. But no one is pressured to take part in any activity.

Don't underestimate the value of fun. Used appropriately, it can make your work day more fun and reduce stress so you can do your job even better. Now that's a good prescription!

TOUGHENING UP THIN SKIN

Though it may not seem so, most personal upset is self-inflicted. External events and people really don't upset us per se. We upset ourselves, according to Albert Ellis, author of *How to Stubbornly Refuse to Make Yourself Miserable about Anything — Yes, Anything!* (Lyle Stuart).

Ellis says it's unfair and unethical to make yourself miserable. Why? Because you hurt the most important person in your life — you — as well as those who like to see you happy. This is not to say you'll never feel mad or disappointed. But irrational anger and depression achieve nothing. Here are tips on how to feel better about yourself:

- Acknowledge what upset you. What did you let bother you?

- Avoid shoulds and musts. Too often, we turn desires and preferences into shoulds and musts. Examples: "I should have made better conversation." "I must improve my analytical skills before this next project." The subsequent stress only upsets us more.

- Question musts. Change them into preferences. Example: "I'd prefer to be promoted next month, but if I'm not, I'll get the skills I need for the next time."

- Think rationally. Set your sights on those things that you actually can achieve. Setting yourself up for disappointment will only make you feel worse.

HOW CRITICISM HURTS (AND HELPS)

How do you respond to criticism? Nobody exactly looks forward to being a critic. But understanding criticism for what it is helps make criticism a positive tool you can use to advance yourself professionally.

The key to accepting criticism is to understand its real value to you and your career. Then, you can learn to use criticism to your advantage. Although it might be hard to believe, constructive criticism is a positive force that can lead to professional improvement and personal growth. We must learn from our mistakes, in fact, to progress in all areas of our lives. So you really can gain through the pain of criticism.

Of course, no one likes to be criticized. It doesn't feel good to have our mistakes pointed out when we're already fully aware of what's gone wrong. But keep this in mind: It's your performance or behavior — and not you as a person — that is being criticized, at least if the criticism is well-intentioned and not personal. So, don't take it personally. View it instead as an opportunity to learn how to improve your performance.

When you can accept criticism, you become a more open and flexible person. You're more willing to listen to other people's ideas and suggestions. Resistance to criticism can go hand-in-hand with an unwillingness to consider anything new or to entertain ideas or concepts that may challenge cherished beliefs and prejudices.

What should you do if you just can't handle criticism well? Try these techniques.

The next time someone criticizes you, see if you can:

- Stay calm and receptive to what's being said. Immediate emotional reactions usually make it hard to understand critical remarks.

- Ask for clarification if you don't understand exactly what you're being criticized for.

- Thank the other person for the feedback. You don't have to make any other response on the spot. You may want to say, "I'd like to talk with you more later, after I've had a chance to think about what you've said."

- Ask yourself, "Is this criticism valid? If so, how am I going to act on it?"

- Consider what you can learn from the feedback and then promise yourself that you'll follow through.

HAVING A HOT HEAD BURNS CREDIBILITY

It can be infuriating. A coworker pushes all your buttons, and you're about to explode. But letting all your anger out will only come back to haunt you. You'll not only blow your top, but you'll also blow your credibility.

The first step toward managing anger in the workplace is to identify what triggers it. It could be:

- Having a boss who regularly criticizes you in front of others

- Having to deal with someone who disrupts meetings and interrupts as you talk

- Having a coworker who refuses to admit mistakes

  These are just a few sources of workplace conflict. You can probably generate your own list. Whatever your particular "triggers," it's important to know how to respond in a work setting. Here are some suggestions:

- Be cool. Don't respond at all, and remain in control. That doesn't mean holding it in. It means dealing with the culprit in private or talking to a nonbusiness friend about the problem.

- Be patient. If you can wait for the right moment to respond, you can clearly direct and channel your anger. You'll be the one in control.

- See the lighter side. If you can step back and put things in a broader perspective, you might try a little humor. It may ease the tension, as long as your humor doesn't imply that you're mocking the other person or taking the problem too lightly.

QUICK TIPS

- **Keep cool about change.** Facing a major change at work, such as a new boss or increased layoffs, can be stressful. Remember how you coped with change in the past and think about how you can use similar strategies now.

- **Strategic lunch plans.** What happens when you eat certain foods at lunch? Do you come back to work refueled and raring to go, or sluggish and ready to sleep? A high-fiber breakfast enables a person to eat less at lunch. Strategize with your stomach to learn what works best for you.

- **Accentuate the positive activity.** Start the day with a task you enjoy. It will put you in a positive frame of mind, ready to tackle all those necessary but perhaps less enjoyable tasks ahead.

- **Tough decision deadline.** When you have a hard choice to make, reduce your stress by setting a timetable: "I will decide to address this issue in the next 15 minutes." Even if you don't *solve* the partiular problem in 15 minutes, you will have taken the first step.

- **Water to the rescue.** If you feel headachy and listless, a big glass of water may help. Dehydration is a bigger problem than most people imagine, according to *Be Well, Work Well* (Dartnell). Aim for six glasses a day.

- **Temperature control.** People have confidence in those who keep their composure under pressure. Even if you feeel you're about to burst with anger or frustration, try to keep cool. People will respect your ability to maintain self-control.

QUIZ

Is All Work and No Play Doing You In?

We all want to do our best at work. Our goals should be to use our time well and devote maximum energy, creativity, and enthusiasm to what we do. Nearly everyone has to put in extra hours from time to time. But when working hard is taken to an extreme, most people cease to perform well, confusing long hours with increased productivity. Eventually the hard pace takes its toll. Are you inclined to be a workaholic? Take the following quiz to find out.

	YES	NO
1. Do you always like to get to work and get started before anyone else?	___	___
2. Do you usually stay at work later than your colleagues do?	___	___
3. Do you often volunteer to take on extra assignments, even if you don't really have the time to do them?	___	___
4. If you're not at work, do you worry that things won't get done without you?	___	___
5. Do you typically think about work on weekends and during vacations?	___	___
6. Do you often forego vacation time to stay on top of your work?	___	___
7. Do you often have trouble sleeping because you're thinking about your job?	___	___
8. Do your coworkers seem unappreciative of the extra time you put in?	___	___
9. Do you always feel that you're falling behind in the tasks you're expected to complete?	___	___
10. Do you often cancel social engagements because you think you have to work late?	___	___

TOTAL NUMBER OF YES ANSWERS: _____

Are you overworked? A score of eight or more Yes answers suggests you display signs of workaholicism. You might be keeping a pace that can ruin you physically and professionally. Remember that it is the quality of your work that is important, not quantity alone. If time management is the problem, see Chapter 10. Otherwise, take more time out for something you enjoy. It may be as simple as reading a book for one hour before going to bed. Don't let work overwhelm you.

YOUR CAREER SURVIVAL TOOL KIT TAKE-AWAY

The 1st tool

Managing stress

In a time of budget cuts and downsizing, stress is greater than ever. It hits from a variety of fronts. With fewer people to help out, we all are doing more work with less help. And with less job security, there is the constant, nagging fear that we may have no job at all tomorrow. The best defense against the pressures and stress of the modern work world is to actively pursue "The 7 Simple Things You *Must* Do To Keep Your Job Today (*And* Tomorrow)" described in Part 1 of this book. That's because when you take your future into your own hands, you have a greater sense of control over your work life, and that helps buffer some of the harmful effects of job stress, according to psychologist James Campbell Quick, a professor and editor of *The Journal of Occupational Health Psychology.*

WHAT YOU CAN DO

- **Don't let angry coworkers or customers get the best of you.** Separate your thoughts from your feelings. Tell the person that there's no reason to yell at you, but avoid yelling back at them. Take a step back and count to ten.

- **Don't lose perspective.** Keeping workplace problems in perspective is one of your best guards against stress, the experts say. "Ask yourself on a scale of 1 to 10 how close this situation is to life and death," advises Joanne Moskowitz, a therapist with the Biofeedback and Stress Management Center of Westchester in White Plains, New York. Then devote your emotional energy to the task accordingly, she says.

- **Change your attitude.** According to a survey by *Vitality* magazine, people who hold up well under stress have three things in common: (1) They view change as a challenge; (2) They have a purpose or goal that inspires them; and (3) they try to maintain control over themselves and their lives. They have also trained themselves to let go of their anger, resentment, and fear. Instead, they express a hearty sense of humor.

- **Develop healthy habits.** A good diet, rest, and exercise are the best remedies known for stress. Regular exercise — especially aerobic — affects the body chemicals that trigger stress, according to psychologist James Campbell Quick.

CHAPTER NINE

Career Survival Tool #2:
TAKING ON TECHNOLOGY

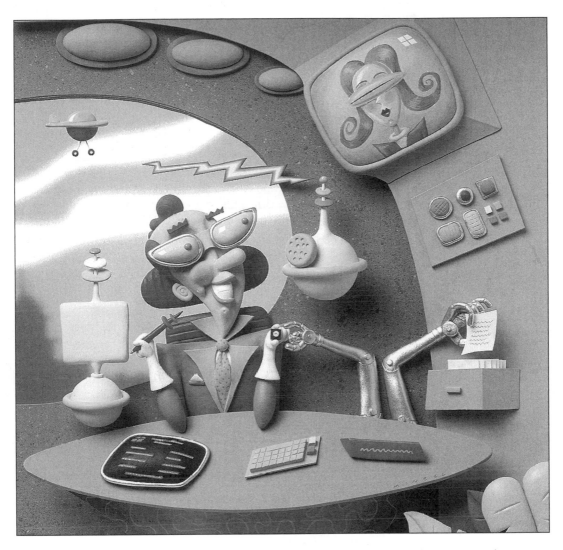

*"Automation may be great, but nothing speeds up work
like a wastebasket."*

— ANONYMOUS

INTRODUCTION

When computers first made their way into the workplace in the 1970s, you could divide most offices in half. On one side, you'd find the employees who *couldn't wait* to turn their computers on. They were curious about all the ways the computer would change the ways they did their jobs. They welcomed the new technology with open arms.

A look of fear dominated the faces of the other workers. They dreaded the new machines. Some kept typewriters on the corner of their desks, perhaps to serve as some kind of security blanket. These workers had no desire to go to computer classes and were scared to death every time they turned on their monitors. They seemed to fight the new technology every step of the way.

It's understandable that some people would be a little leery of computers at first. The new machines meant a radical change from the way things had been done before. But the sad truth is, unless those employees overcame their fears and opened their minds to all the potential uses they could get from the newfangled equipment — if they didn't embrace technology — they became dinosaurs. The modern workplace — with its high-tech voice answering systems, fax machines, laptop computers, modems, and all the rest — simply left those employees behind.

The lesson from that era couldn't be more clear: the technological world waits for no one. The only way to remain a valuable commodity in the workplace of the future is to keep up with technology. It's as simple as that.

Your willingness to take on technology is the second valuable tool in your Career Survival Tool Kit. As you'll discover in the pages that follow, taking on technology *doesn't* mean you need to know everything about every new software program out there. It *does* mean that you do your best to be well informed about technological trends, that you constantly explore new (and time and cost saving) uses for the technology you're using today, and that you remain open to all the new changes that come your way.

Don't kid yourself into complacency because you've "aced" the office computer. Your willingness to learn the skills you needed to use the computer is a good sign. But change is constant, and unless you forge right ahead with it, something new will leave *you* behind the next time. Embrace today's technology, but keep your eye focused on the future.

WHAT WOULD YOU DO?

CALLERS ARE MORE IMPATIENT THAN EVER!

*Y*ou only put a caller on hold for 15 seconds — it couldn't have been a second more — yet he gave you the hardest time possible about it! What is it with customers? They'll wait an hour in line at Disneyland, but they won't wait on hold for 15 seconds!

In survey after survey, the biggest complaint callers have about calling businesses is having to wait on hold. Brenda, a telephone customer service rep for more than a decade, blames the increasing impatience on better technology and improved telephone service. "Today, callers expect to be taken care of immediately if not sooner," she says. "They used to be a bit more patient."

Naturally, the best solution is to never put callers on hold. But anyone who has worked on the telephone for more than five minutes knows this isn't possible. So, when you have to put a caller on hold, always ask his or her permission. That will help callers feel like they have some control over the situation.

Could you be compounding the problem by not being sensitive to how callers feel about being put on hold, asks Victoria Stevens, a manufacturing assistant at BC Manufacturing, Inc, Blue Springs, Missouri. "As consumers, most of us get uptight when we've been put on what seems the never ending hold, even though the amount of time actually spent holding is shorter than what it seems," she says.

Stevens suggests this experiment: "Have a coworker put you on a hold line, and then have him or her keep track of the amount of time you're holding. "As you are on the line, examine your feelings about being on hold. Then stop and compare. Tell your coworker how long it seemed you were on hold. The time you actually were waiting most likely will be less than you estimated," she says.

So, even though you may put someone on hold only for a short time, human nature is such that it can seem like an eternity to that caller. Once you relate your holding experience with what the person is going through, you'll probably do your best to keep the wait short for callers.

Be sure to check back with the caller every 20 to 25 seconds while he or she is holding, says Stevens. "Let the caller know you're still working on the problem." If the caller doesn't want to keep holding, get the person's number and call back as soon as you have tracked down the information you need.

Finally, after returning to the call, always express your appreciation: "Thank you for waiting." Your gracious words may help defuse any anger the customer may have built up while on hold.

COMMON PHONE PEEVES

A recent survey asked 564 businesspeople what bothers them most about how a business phone is answered. Their responses:

- 42 percent cited automated phone menus.
- 34 percent mentioned being put on hold without being asked first.
- 30 percent noted employees who are uninformed about the subject of their call.

People's perceptions of you and your company often are formed the minute you answer the phone. Use that minute well.

A CYNIC PUTS TECHNOLOGY IN ITS PLACE

Technology enhances workplace productivity, says journalist Michael Schrage, but the human factor is far more important. Here are highlights of an exclusive interview with the syndicated columnist and author of *Shared Minds* (Random House), a book espousing technology to help people work together.

Q: **Has technology improved productivity?**

A: Not that much. Believing information management to be the key to success in the Information Age, businesses invested millions in high tech. Now, well into the computer revolution, statistics show minimal gains in productivity.

Q: **Why?**

A: The assumption of the importance of information management is wrong. Companies and workers don't create success by managing information, but by managing relationships with customers.

Q: **Why are some people afraid of technology?**

A: People aren't fools. Sure, they can push 50 buttons and create wonderful reports, but they know it's the quality of relationships that determines success. Is the customer getting what he wants? Information and relationships must be balanced. Too often, we maximize one over the other.

Nobody is threatened by picking up the phone or sending a fax. But if workers or customers are told, "We don't want to talk — just send e-mail messages," they get jittery. A person becomes data. Is this how a customer should feel?

Q: **What's your central complaint about high tech?**

A: The emphasis on individual productivity turns offices into private ghettos where workers just "process" data. Give people tools to work on their own, but also facilitate sharing, jointly creating with others.

Q: **How about an example?**

A: A salesperson uses a laptop computer with a client to "customize" a product the customer wants. Some companies have "hold jockeys" to chat with customers waiting to talk with an expert. It's a smart way of "humanizing" the wait.

Q: **What's the key measure of workplace technology?**

A: How you use it to create value. Voice mail creates value by allowing customers to avoid telephone tag or to make requests that don't require a conversation. Fax machines speed purchase orders or designs that need quick approval.

Q: **Any more advice?**

A: Never neglect the person-to-person relationship. Provide easy access to a human being.

Do You Hide Behind Voice Mail?

After several bad experiences with a distributor, George Rawson had to call the customer service rep to say his company would not renew its contract. "I like this rep," says Rawson. "I don't blame her. So I was not looking forward to making the call." And call he did. But instead of reaching the rep, Rawson reached voice mail. "I have to admit, I breathed a sigh of relief," he says. "It was much easier delivering the bad news through voice mail than actually talking to her."

E-mail, answering machines, and voice mail. New technology has lessened the need for face-to-face or even voice-to-voice contact. These tools designed for convenience have created less human communication.

The problem is not a new one. In fact, early developers of the telephone suspected it would be used only for business. They doubted people would want to talk socially on the telephone because it wasn't face-to-face.

With even greater electronic distancing since those first phones comes the danger that we will begin treating people less like human beings. Phone reps, who talk to countless customers every day but may never see one, can also let courtesy take a backseat to technology.

Marcia, a bank customer service supervisor, encourages reps to go to the lobby, "just to remind them that there are real human beings behind those account numbers," she says.

How can you be sure you aren't letting technology take the "people" out of your everyday communication? Here are some helpful suggestions:

- Keep it personal. Technology may build distances, but those distances are not insurmountable. "If you have customers you deal with regularly, take time out of each call to include a personal question or comment," suggests Rosanne Miles, a Chicago-area consultant who provides phone skills training. "Follow up the next time you talk. That not only makes customers feel good, but it helps you keep your perspective in check."

At a utility company's billing center, a bulletin board is covered with photographs and letters from customers for just that purpose.

- Respond to electronic messages. "Nothing creates a bigger distance than the feeling that a business is hiding behind its technology," says Miles. Respond quickly and you use technology to serve better, not to set up barriers with your customers and coworkers.

Voice-mail systems, says Miles, should include an option for reaching the operator. "You don't want customers bumped around by mechanical voices." Also, when you leave electronic messages, let customers know how to reach you in person. "You maintain the human connection when you give them the choice of speaking to you," says Miles.

- Keep technology in perspective. "Remember, technology is only a tool," explains Miles. "It's meant to help you serve customers better, quicker, and more efficiently. But the technology is not the final word. Use it so it serves you, not the other way around."

TIME IS RIGHT FOR NEW IMPROVED VOICE-MAIL MESSAGE

Is your voice-mail message as old as your system? If so, it's time to update it. Be sure your new message includes these key elements:

- Today's date. To really show you're on top of your voice mail, change the message daily: "Today is Monday, November 1, and I'll be in the office all day."

- Your availability. Unless you indicate otherwise, most callers assume you will return their call within an hour or two. If you're out of the office or expect to be stuck in a meeting most of the morning, say so in your message.

- How callers can leave a message. Most know to "wait until after the tone." Today, you need only let callers know of unusual requirements, such as entering a particular tone to leave a fax, or to warn of limited message time.

- How to reach someone else. Always provide callers a means for reaching someone else if they cannot wait for a return call from you: "To speak with someone immediately, press pound 235."

'PRESS ONE' IF YOU REGRET PLACING THIS CALL

In a recent survey, executives from the nation's largest companies said 40 percent of the voice-mail systems they reach are annoying or hard to use. "If properly used, voice mail is an effective tool," says Robert Half, founder of Accountemps, the temporary agency that commissioned the study. "Unfortunately, some systems take several minutes to navigate

ACTION IDEA

Keep it personal.

• Answer one e-mail message this week with a personal visit to your coworkers' work area.

• Try to answers calls personally today. Don't let any bounce to voice mail.

• Block out one hour a day to be at your desk taking calls. When you leave messages for others, let them know the time you expect to be available — "live" — to talk to them.

because of a plethora of options, many of which may seem unrelated to a caller's individual query."

"Voice mail should not be used to replace communication. Whenever possible, callers should ultimately be able to talk to an actual person, especially if it is a service-related business," suggests Half.

VOICE-MAIL MESSAGES THAT GET RESULTS

Voice mail — these days everyone's got it and sometimes it seems as though everybody hates it. Most of us probably would prefer to speak to another human being, but perhaps what gripes us most about voice mail is not getting a timely response to the messages we leave for others.

"If you feel your voice-mail messages too often are given low priority, it may be time to assess the quality of those messages," says Margo Chevers, president of Northeast Leadership Enterprise of Plainville, Massachusetts. Chevers, who also is the author of *Stop the (B)ad (S)ervice* (Kendall Hunt Publishing Co.), emphasizes that "you need to make it easy and convenient for others to return your calls."

She herself dreads receiving voice-mail messages such as, "Hi, Margo, this is Bob Smith. We talked three months ago; give me a call." "I would have no idea what company Bob Smith is with, what the circumstances of our initial meeting were, or what we apparently talked about," Chevers points out.

If you expect people to return your calls in response to your voice-mail messages, Chevers suggests you include this basic information:

- Your company's name, in addition to your own.

- The reason you are calling. This includes information that will help the other person "place" you. For example, if you ate lunch at a conference with the person you are trying to reach, you might say, "I met you last month at the ABC conference and we had lunch together on the last day. I told you that I would get back to you with information about my company's marketing plan."

- Information you need that the other person can research before returning your call. If you are calling with a complaint, for example, give details that include the specific product or service about which you are complaining, the reason for your concerns, and what action you expect to be taken.

- Your telephone number. "You may get a return call more quickly if you leave a number, saving the other person the bother of having to look for it," Chevers says. Don't assume that the people you call have your phone number at their fingertips. Many people access their voice mailboxes when they are away from their offices. Keep in mind, too, that people don't always keep the telephone numbers they collect at business events.

• Times when you can be reached. This information helps you avoid playing "telephone tag" with the other party

Chevers also offers these tips for leaving voice-mail messages:

• Indicate the urgency of your call. Do you need an immediate return call, or can it wait? "When we're away from the office, most of us appreciate a voice-mail message that helps us prioritize our return calls," she says.

• Keep your message brief. "People will tune out if your message is too long," warns Chevers, who speaks from experience. "One individual leaves me 15-minute messages, which I do not want to listen to," she explains. "While it's important to leave enough information, you should respect other people's time by providing only necessary information."

• Learn from others' mistakes. Do you sometimes find yourself gritting your teeth over messages left on your voice mail? Perhaps they're too long-winded, inexact, or so rapidly delivered that you can't understand the recording.

Take note of what you find annoying, and be sure you don't get into the same bad habits when you leave voice-mail messages for others.

CONTROL COSTLY COMMUNICATION

Before making that next phone call, or sending that next fax, pause and ask yourself: "Is this the least expensive way I can do this?" That request comes from your boss.

According to a survey of Fortune 500 companies by Pitney Bowes Management Services, more than 70 percent of managers responsible for communication costs at large companies say employees often use costly services improperly.

The most costly charges:

• Making local calls for personal reasons

• Using internal fax instead of interoffice delivery

• Use of overnight delivery instead of 2- to 3-day delivery

• Use of overnight instead of first-class mail

"Most employees aren't deliberately running up unnecessary charges," explains San Francisco-based management consultant Tyler Hall. "Because they're under pressure to work fast, they're just rushing to do what is quicker or more convenient."

Hall suggests making sure you are aware of all your options before using a communication service. For example, "Talk to mailroom personnel about sending options," he explains. "I know of one secretary who had no idea a package could be sent by 2- or 3-day delivery at a much lower rate," he says.

Know the differences in costs and be prepared to justify costs compared to need. "Certainly, there are times you must fax a document across the country immediately," says Hall. "But how often do we fax documents that could have been sent by mail for 32 cents and saved several dollars in long-distance costs?"

Also, become familiar with your technology. Hall says many offices save money by programming the fax machine to send less-urgent faxes out overnight. "Everybody learned how to use the fax, but to use it *well*, you have to take your education to the next level."

THE E-MAIL ADVANTAGE

Quicker than you can turn on your computer, electronic mail (e-mail) is gaining popularity as a form of business communication. And as more professionals gain access to e-mail, they are finding more and more ways to use it. For example:

- At Iowa Electric Light and Power, manager Mary Benfield writes a daily "Morning Report" via e-mail for all the customer service center team members. It contains a motivational message, such as "When we have done our best, we should await the results in peace."

- At Eccentric Software in Corvallis, Oregon, e-mail and on-line services have proven to be the best methods of encouraging productivity among its teams. "We run a virtual office in which most of our contractors work from home, sometimes over several time zones," says David Goldstein, manager. "E-mail is the most efficient means of communication under these kinds of circumstances."

- At Hewlett-Packard, the organization's 97,000 employees exchange 20 million e-mail messages each month. "With the ability to share information broadly and fully, without filtering it through a hierarchy, we can manage the way we always wanted to," says Robert Walker, chief information officer.

This all sounds very good. But, by its very nature, e-mail eliminates personal contact. Is it good for teamwork? "Yes," says Northwestern University's Joseph Walther, Ph.D., a professor of communications studies. Communicating with teammates electronically leads to quality decision making, especially for complex, long-term projects, he says. The big advantage to communicating by e-mail is that colleagues can work together despite different schedules and locations, Walther says.

Another plus is that electronic communication forces peers to go on record with their concerns. "You can't register your disagreement by rolling your eyes if no one is there to see you," says Walther. "You're compelled to say in words just what you think." And making disagreements explicit, he says, leads to better joint decisions.

Communicating by computer also has interpersonal benefits. In one study, Walther assigned a series of decision-making tasks to 16 groups meeting face-to-face and 16 groups working exclusively by e-mail. Six weeks later, the groups that conferred by computer were more socially oriented than those meeting in person. Walther found that group members took time to compare hobbies, discuss music, and talk sports.

In *Psychology Today*, Walther coins the term "hyperpersonal communication" to describe this type of teamwork because computer users became closer than nonusers.

Forging social connections by e-mail may take longer than in person, but there is a payoff. The bonds it forms can help colleagues reach a consensus — and that's a key goal of any collaboration.

WHO'S READING YOUR E-MAIL? MAYBE THE BOSS

Sure, you use a password to access your e-mail. But don't assume that your e-mail messages are private.

When Michael A. Smyth sent an e-mail message in 1994 to a coworker, calling his employers "backstabbing bas——," he had little concern that someone else was reading what he thought was a private message. After all, hadn't the company promised him that e-mail communications would remain confidential?

They weren't. Executives at his company saw the message, and Smyth was dismissed for what the company deemed "inappropriate and unprofessional comments." In Smyth's "wrongful dismissal" suit, the company claimed it never told Smyth his messages were private. A Federal court dismissed Smyth's case saying that even if the company had promised confidentiality, the "defendant's actions did not tortuously invade the plaintiff's privacy."

Employers are increasingly viewing employee e-mail messages as "company property" because that is how the courts are viewing the messages.

In a landmark case, Merrill Lynch had to pay $2 million in punitive damages because one of its brokers conducted fraudulent trading over the company's e-mail system. Even though the employee was fired when the company found out about it, the court found that the firm had a duty to control and regulate information that had originated with the company and was sent over the network.

E-mail records are being used in other cases as well. As a result, e-mail administrators can, and often do, monitor the messages sent on the system. And, depending on your system's software and configuration, e-mail messages may be stored on a backup system, even after users have deleted them.

John Jessen is a Seattle "computer detective" who searches through computer disk drives and network servers for evidence that strengthens his clients' cases in court. Jessen's recommendation: "Don't put anything in e-mail that you wouldn't want read over the loudspeaker throughout the company. ... You are creating a permanent record of something that might be dragged up at a later point." Even if you are 100 percent certain that no one monitors your e-mail, there's still reason to watch what you write. Think of how easy it is to click on the wrong receiver's name and send your message to the wrong person.

E-Mail Etiquette

Next time you're writing an e-mail message, keep in mind that, like written, telephone, or face-to-face communication, electronic correspondence requires common rules of courtesy and etiquette (or "netiquette"):

- Always be businesslike. A good rule of thumb is to never say anything in an e-mail message that you wouldn't say face to face.

- Carefully consider who needs to receive your message. With e-mail address groups, a simple click of the mouse can send a message to an entire department or organization. But should you? It's inconsiderate and inefficient to transmit a message to an entire address group if it really needs to go to only two or three people.

  If you respond to a message that has been distributed to a group, think carefully about whether you need to reply only to the sender of the message or to everyone who received it.

- Keep messages brief and to the point. E-mail is supposed to speed up communication, not slow it down.

- Answer your messages promptly. If you have to check out some information, dash off a quick e-mail, letting the sender know you received his or her message and when you will have the information requested.

- Avoid sending personal messages. It's bad to use office e-mail for personal communication. Employers frown on the practice — they see it as a modern day version of gossiping around the office water cooler.

- Be careful about sending confidential messages. The contents of the message may wind up in the hands of someone you don't want reading it.

Surfing, Saving on The Net

Many people want to explore the Internet or World Wide Web but are hesitant because it seems so big, confusing, and overwhelming. But don't let the Internet daunt you. Taking the time to "play" and "surf" the Internet is the best way to find out what on-line services are available.

But online services cost money and the tolls add up while you are aimlessly searching the system. Becky Seeger, a program assistant in the

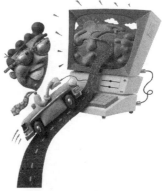

Action Idea

Once you began using e-mail, you probably noticed how much time it could save for you. But has your use of e-mail "leveled out"? That is, have you stopped trying to develop new ways to use e-mail to further improve your productivity? Try this today: Think of at least one new way you can begin using e-mail. Implement it immediately.

News Bureau at the University of Wisconsin, Eau Claire, offers these tips in *Creative Secretary's Letter* for efficient use of on-line services:

- Plan ahead. Before you start surfing, decide exactly what information you want from the service.

- Use good judgment. If you're having problems with new software, your computer service department may be able to provide cheaper assistance than you can get on-line.

- Know what you're doing. Learn how to travel on-line to avoid unproductive — but costly — surfing excursions.

THERE'S NO GUARANTEE AGAINST COMPUTER VIRUSES

Computer viruses are a real danger, but it's almost impossible to avoid every circumstance where your computer may contract one. Instead of letting fear limit how you use your corrupter and modem, look at ways to avoid viruses and eliminate them when they hit.

Your computer can get infected with a virus if you run a program that is infected. You can get infected files from just about any source: files you've copied from a friend, floppy or hard disk programs you've downloaded from bulletin boards and other online sources, or even from brand-new commercial software.

In her book *Telecom Made Easy* (Aegis), June Langhoff offers these general guidelines to protect your computer from viruses:

- Don't download programs (or files with attached programs) from bulletin boards that are not familiar to you.

- Don't buy or use pirated software.

- Back up your hard disk regularly.

- When someone you don't know sends you an e-mail, don't download or open the attached file. (You can't get viruses from reading the e-mail alone.)

There are all kinds of viruses, and some can remain hidden in your system for months or years. How do you know if you have a virus? Here are some of the most common symptoms:

- Your system date and time stamp changes all by itself.

- You notice that your programs have been growing in size.

- Your system is crashing more often.

- Your computer seems to be slowing down.

- You get weird error messages, such as "Feed me" or "Haha."

- Your disk is wiped clean.

Most on-line services are well protected from viruses. For your own computer, your best bet is to install an antivirus program. These programs scan your hard disk and each floppy disk before you copy files to your computer and before you run the programs they contain.

You can keep your antivirus program up-to-date by subscribing to the program's update service. Updated monthly programs are preferable to annual programs.

Although the risk of contracting a computer virus is very real, it shouldn't limit your ability to explore cyberspace. Just make sure you use common sense and good judgment — and invest in a solid virus-protection program.

IMPROVE SERVICE WITH FAX-ON-DEMAND

For more than a decade, the fax machine has been part of business communications. Now, increasing numbers of small and large companies are taking fax technology to the next level to improve their ability to serve customers. How? Through fax-on-demand (FOD):

What is fax-on-demand? A customer calls an advertised number (often toll free), listens to a menu of choices, keys in a one- to five-digit number to request a particular document, and enters the fax number to which the document should be sent. Moments later, the fax is on its way.

Do customers like fax-on-demand? According to the authors of *Fax-on-Demand: Marketing Tool of the '90s* (Berkley), callers given the option of receiving information from an electronic bulletin board or via fax have selected fax delivery by a margin of 3-to-1.

How would we use fax-on-demand to serve our customers? In *Telecom Made Easy* (Aegis), Langhoff lists a number of ways companies can utilize FOD technology to serve customers and clients:

- Mail-order companies can fax individual pages from their catalogs, brochures, and price sheets to callers requesting information.

- Hardware and software firms can promote technical support via fax.

- Booksellers can fax back catalog information, or even the first page of a new thriller, to encourage customers to place an order.

- Real estate agents can set up a system that briefly describes each property. The caller makes a selection, and the system faxes a floor plan, photo, and/or marketing flier.

What do we need to get fax-on-demand started in our office? To set up an FOD system, you need a dedicated computer, a dedicated phone line, a voice/fax board, and software that supports FOD. You can get systems that will work on only one phone line, but many require at least two. Some systems enable the sender to pay for the outgoing fax call, and some — mostly the more expensive systems — take credit card orders.

FOD systems range in price from $500 to over $15,000. The higher-priced systems come pre-installed on their own computer and have many features.

If you aren't sure if FOD will work for you, consider a trial run first. You can contact an FOD service provider who will take care of all the details. They are listed in the Yellow Pages under "Fax transmission services."

We have FOD. How can we get word out to our customers about what we have available by fax? When customers request information, offer it by mail. But always be sure to mention the FOD option. They will appreciate being told about the opportunity to obtain information in such a timely manner.

BRAINSTORMING BY FAX

A key project needs brainstorming with your colleagues at several different branches. Unfortunately, conflicting schedules make teleconferencing impractical, there is no universal e-mail connecting branches, and budgets won't allow travel. Before office automation, this problem might have proved especially difficult. But your friendly office fax machine can help you carry out a long-distance brainstorming session. Here's how:

The "project leader" outlines the issue at hand and faxes the first person on an established routing list. That person adds comments and suggestions on the page and faxes to the next person. The fax travels to all the usual participants, hitting each during business hours.

Within 24 hours, the "round-robin" fax is back to the originator, who selects an idea to end the session or starts the process again.

Problem solved!

ACTION IDEA

Sure, you're courteous on the telephone. But do you show the same courtesy when you send faxes?

People who receive faxes care about two things: Are they readable? and How long do the transmissions tie up the fax line?

Avoid sending materials with fancy typographical elements and graphics. They devour transmission time and often break up upon printing. And be careful about faxing photographs, says Bob Hill of News/Broadcast Network: "What comes across looks like nighttime in a coal mine."

QUICK TIPS

- **Hope for the dozing callers.** Callers go into "auto-doze" if they have to listen to more than five or six options when they reach a voice-mail system. Keep the menu short!

- **Have phone, will travel safer.** Don't feel guilty about having a cellular phone. A cellular phone is one of the best defenses against crime, says a Chicago police detective who speaks to community groups about crime prevention. "These are no longer the toy of an executive. They're a tool — like a spare tire," says Detective J.J. Bittenbinder.

- **... Or maybe not so safely!** The attention of drivers using car phones is reduced by 20 percent or more, according to a study by the Automobile Foundation for Traffic Safety. Pull over!

- **Spend more time on line.** If you aren't familiar with the Internet, check it out. More than 78 percent of businesses surveyed for 3M Corporation said they expect to increase the use of on-line services or the Internet in the next year. That probably includes your organization.

- **Frequent use of fax features.** Fewer than 8 percent of fax users use the advanced features on their machines, one manufacturer estimates. *Handy and often overlooked:* auto retry, which keeps dialing until the connection is made.

- **Know the code.** Most states now have more than one area code (at last count California had 14!); as available phone numbers are used up, more areas will be adding area codes. So even though you think you know a customer's area code, it's important to ask. When a customer calls in, be sure to check the code and update your records.

QUIZ

Are Your Skills Up to the Minute?

"I work in the customer service department of a computer software company. Sometimes, I feel like I can't keep up with all our new upgrades as well as all the changes in our industry as a whole. Am I overreacting, or am I really being left behind?"

— *M.K.F, St. Louis, Missouri*

The marketplace is in flux like never before — not just in your industry, but everywhere. Every day there is something new: new products, new strategies, new technological advances. Where does that leave you: behind or ahead of the game? Take this simple quiz to find out.

	YES	NO
1. Are you up-to-date on all of your company's product and service revisions?	___	___
2. Equally important, are you up-to-date on your competitor's revisions?	___	___
3. Are you conversant with the latest developments in your industry?	___	___
4. Are you familiar with your key customers' important business plans?	___	___
5. Do you keep abreast of current selling techniques and strategies?	___	___
6. Do you follow the trade press to keep up with executive changes in your field?	___	___
7. Do you always know who is moving in and out of your field?	___	___
8. Are you a computer-friendly person?	___	___
9. Are your call reports automated?	___	___
10. Do you have regular access to competitive intelligence sources?	___	___

TOTAL NUMBER OF YES ANSWERS_____

Are you being left behind? Winners in this test are those who "concentrate on the affirmative." Nine or 10 Yes answers rank you as a super pro. Seven or eight rate you fair to good. Any score below seven indicates you may be behind the times a bit, and your work is cut out for you. But don't be overwhelmed. Just make a commitment to yourself to spend some time every week updating yourself on new developments.

YOUR CAREER SURVIVAL TOOL KIT TAKE-AWAY
The 2nd tool

Taking on technology

The more *you* use your computer, the better your boss is paid. And the more *your boss* uses her computer, the more money you make.

That's the interesting finding of a recent study by two professors at the Wharton School of the University of Pennsylvania. Adjusting for factors like the educational background of the workforce, the professors found that the earnings of production workers increased 3 percent annually when their managers' use of computers doubled. Only half the increase was attributed to greater worker skills. The study suggests that the introduction of computers into a company frees its employees to take on more complicated duties.

Managers benefited even more. Their earnings climbed by 3.5 percent when the production workers doubled their use of computers.

The study confirms that you make yourself more indispensable in the workplace by knowing all you can about technology. If bosses are making more money when their workforce is well-versed on computers, they're more likely to hire those employees who can utilize technology to its fullest potential. That's why taking on technology is a valuable tool in your Career Survival Tool Box.

WHAT YOU CAN DO

- **Find *one new use* for your computer and begin using it.** It may be something as simple as a new time management software program or the computer "timer" feature. By searching the computer program manager, one secretary discovered that her office computer was equipped with a desk calendar. She found that by simply blocking in appointments she was increasing her efficiency and lowering the level of stress she felt each day.

- **Read at least one computer magazine each month.** There are publications for every level of computer literacy. A magazine like *PC Novice* is geared for the most basic computer user. As your knowledge increases, move up to more challenging publications.

- **Try one of the on-line services.** America Online, CompuServe, and other services are very user-friendly. And now that they offer simple Internet access, there's no excuse for not surfing the Internet, a world that was once accessible only to the most sophisticated on-line traveler.

- **Get more use out of your office telephone.** Sounds fairly elementary, doesn't it? But the fact is, most people had only the most basic training on their office phone systems. As a result, they use the few features they absolutely need to make and receive calls. But if you check out the manual, or ask human resources for some help, you'll probably discover at least several new features that can save you time and trouble. For example, one manager was surprised to learn he could send a single voice-mail message to more than one party. Prior to discovering that feature, he'd repeat the same message in the voice mailbox of each of his five staff members.

CHAPTER TEN

Career Survival Tool #3:
CONQUERING TIME MANAGEMENT

"I have noticed that the people who are late are often so much jollier than the people who have to wait for them."

— E.V. LUCAS (1868–1938), ENGLISH AUTHOR

INTRODUCTION

Is time management a problem for many people? If the number of books that have been published on the subject is any indication, time management is a big problem for many people. In fact, after computer books, then time management is probably *the* "hottest" topic in business book publishing.

Andy Cianni, a Madison, Wisconsin-based time management consultant, is amused that time management is such a big issue. "I shouldn't complain," he says, "because it's my bread and butter. But with all the books out there, and with all these executives and their desk diaries, and now, these computer programs to help you manage time, you would think people would have a better grip on time, but they don't."

Cianni scoffs at the idea that the fast pace of the 1990s makes time management a bigger problem than ever before. "Every generation thinks they are busier and more overwhelmed than the last," he says. "Remember, Dale Carnegie was writing about time management 50 years ago. And even Benjamin Franklin had a few words to say about time."

The problem, Cianni says, is perception. "We all feel we are stuck in a demanding world that is spinning further out of control," he says. "Calendars, desk diaries, to-do lists — they all give us a sense of control. We need these devices and guides psychologically because when we have no control over events, we feel crushed by them."

Gaining control over how you use time is a skill that makes you more indispensable to your current and future employers, Cianni says. "When managers see you making an effort to manage your time, they will view you as disciplined. They like having on their team employees who are constantly striving to improve and who are trying to use their time in the most effective manner …. In fact, they're probably envious of you."

The material in the pages that follow explore a variety of ways you can gain an edge on time. Add these techniques to your Career Survival Tool Kit, and you'll position yourself as the kind of employee no organization can afford to be without.

WHAT WOULD YOU DO?

AVOIDING THE PAPER FLOOD

*H*elp! *Your work area is being swamped by paper. How can you stem the flood of notes, memos, and documents?*

The so-called "paperless office" we were promised at the start of the computer age has grown into a paper monster that devours precious time and space. A few tips for taming it:

- Don't print it — unless you have to. Many documents can be stored in your electronic files without duplication in paper files. Keeping both traditional and electronic files is a key reason for paper proliferation.

- Say it in person. When possible, meet in person for brief discussions of specific issues or concerns that require quick action or decisions. A brief telephone call can eliminate the need for a three-page letter full of unnecessary background.

- Be concise. Proper planning using outlines can lead to a two-page rather than a 10-page report, for example. Promise yourself never to write down a memo of more than one page and keep that promise.

- Route fewer reports. Who really needs to receive one? Check with recipients every six months or so. Do they want or need to continue on the routing list? If you get no response, cut them off.

FREE YOURSELF FROM INFORMATION OVERLOAD

What can you do when your work space becomes inundated with information you don't need? Start digging yourself out from under and be ruthless about unloading unnecessary items, advises Lynn Lively, a Seattle-based speaker on workplace decision making.

"The secret to not being overwhelmed by useless information is to keep what you actually need in a place where you can easily get at it," Lively recommends. Then put everything else where it won't "haunt" you. "Some items can be filed, but a lot of other material can simply be discarded, especially if it's out-of-date," she says.

More suggestions for controlling the volume and quality of information around you:

- Let go of low-priority information. "Most of us have piles of the 'I wish I had time to read this' type of paper, cluttering our work spaces," Lively observes. "We pile up all those reports of committees we don't sit on, for example, hoping that someday we'll read them."

- Don't be an expert in all areas. "Sometimes you just have to say, 'I don't know' or 'I don't have an opinion on that,'" Lively points out.

ACTION IDEA

Make sure you aren't contributing to the information glut. "Think twice before you send a copy of a document — e-mail or hard copy — to someone," Lively advises.

The next time you're sending a document, ask yourself:

- *Does the individual really need it?*

- *Why would you send a copy?*

- *What's the downside of not sending one? To avoid causing offense, it's a good idea to check with people before you drop them from your mailing list.*

"But you can put people in touch with others whose job it is to be an expert in those areas: 'I don't have that information, but you might want to check with Peter. There's a very good chance he'll know.'"

• Develop retention schedules for documents. Retaining outdated material — often for years — keeps many people awash in a sea of useless paper.

• Never spend prime time on low-priority material. You may want to skim certain items, just to keep yourself informed, or to find the nugget or two of information that's important to you. "You can skim old reports, for example, on your lunch break," says Lively, "or while you're waiting for a meeting to start. But spend your prime time reading only information you really need to know."

• Reduce the information coming in. "Make an effort to be taken off other people's distribution lists," advises Lively. If you don't need what they're sending you, try to make sure it doesn't land on your desk in the first place.

"Of course, you might worry about missing something," she acknowledges. "But when you're swamped with a lot of resource material you don't need, you're much more likely to miss something that's really important — probably because you can't find it."

OVERWHELMED? HOW TO CURE A TIME CRUNCH

Do you consistently put in 12-hour days, yet feel guilty that much is left undone? If your life is running on fast-forward, you're not alone.

Joe Cullinane, president of a consulting firm that designs programs to help sales teams become more effective, frequently works long hours to meet deadlines. In between, he sandwiches in an enormous stack of reading.

"We're seeing a convergence of technologies and appliances," Cullinane says. "Computers, teleconferencing, multimedia, and cable TV are all coming together. I need to keep my finger on the pulse of four or five industries I didn't have to before. "

Pat Hayden, senior communications director for a large, nonprofit social services agency, says she routinely juggles the dual demands of getting information out to the public and learning new skills, such as desktop publishing, which might enable her to do her job better. "I don't think anybody has enough time to get everything done," Hayden says.

Many Americans today feel that they are overworked. But are they? Not necessarily, says management consultant Jeff Davidson. He believes we can handle the additional 79 minutes tacked onto our workday over that of our European counterparts. It's everything else competing for our attention that bogs us down. "Feeling overwhelmed always exacerbates feeling overworked," Davidson said in a speech before the U.S. Treasury Executive Institute.

Nearly every aspect of our lives has become more complex. At the office, we deal with downsizings, budget reductions, and the pressure to do more with less. Outside, the staggering population growth has gridlocked the resources of our cities, highways, and airports. Yes, it takes you longer to get to work and, no, the congestion is not going to subside soon.

The following tips will help you gain greater control over your life:

- Stop trying to do it all. The notion of keeping up with everything is illusory and self-defeating, says Davidson. "The sooner you give it up, the better you'll feel and function."

- Be a wise information consumer. Like too much food, too much information is not easily digested. Strike a balance between keeping up and tuning out.

- Use positive imagery. Try this simple exercise: Imagine your workday tomorrow. Create a mental picture of yourself confidently making decisions, enjoying a nutritious lunch, finishing projects, and walking out in the evening with a sense of accomplishment.

- Limit your choices. Learn to recognize the difference between high- and low-level decisions. Refuse to spend much time on the less important choices. If tennis racquets come with brown or black handles, take the one the salesclerk hands you. Keep your mind clear for more important things.

Remember, we all can accomplish amazing feats while working under pressure. And sometimes just getting through your day productively without having a stress attack can be amazing indeed. Take control when you can, and then go with the flow.

GET THE JOB DONE: PLAN AND PRIORITIZE

At work, it seems we always have several things to do simultaneously. But, it is impossible to accomplish everything at once. Goodrich & Sherwood Associates, Inc., a New York-based management consulting firm, offers the following suggestions for getting things done:

- Do only one job at a time.

- Write out a general priority list of all projects and deadlines, and assess the importance of each to you, your manager, and your company. This will guide you to get priorities completed first.

- Group your telephone calls to avoid having an entire day punctuated by endless phone interruptions.

- Arrange your paperwork and desk neatly, so you can easily check the high-priority items and tasks that can be grouped. The time spent planning a day's work will save you more time than the planning tasks take.

ACTION IDEA

Declare a personal Do it! day to finish little, unpleasant, or boring tasks and mark it on your calendar, suggests Effiel Cook, a productivity expert based in Bedford, Massachusetts. Do It! day could be the time to finish one or two larger tasks or several smaller, "must do eventually" ones.

If this catch-up system works for you, Cook recommends a monthly Do It! day to help you stay caught up. "Pick one day each month, mark it on your calendar, and then do it," she advises. "That's what I call working smarter, but not harder."

MUCH ADO ABOUT TO-DO LISTS

Have you seen them? They're everywhere — calendars, notebooks, pads of paper of every size and color — and they're all labeled "to do." What's all the fuss about? Don't most of us list daily tasks and scratch them off as they are completed? Perhaps so, but that's not the most effective use for these great inventions.

Your to-do list can be the key to a more efficient and productive day. Here are some suggestions to show you how:

- What size is best? Whatever size or shape appeals to you is fine. Just make sure that you have enough room to make marginal notes on follow-ups or changes in priorities. Develop a file to save your lists for future reference.

- Prioritize. You probably already make a list of tasks that you must get done (or at least begin) that day. However, prioritizing these tasks is critical. Which tasks absolutely must be completed today? Put those in Category A. What jobs would you like to get done if you have time? Put those in Category B. Establish a third category for tasks that should be done sometime soon, but can slide for a few days if necessary. Now take that category marked A and prioritize those tasks in order of urgency. Do the same for the B and C groups as well. Certainly you want to tackle the first agenda item in group A right away.

- Count down on list items. As you complete each task, check it off or highlight it with a highlighting marker. Don't cross it out with a pen because you might want to refer to it in the future. To do that, you have to be able to read it. Any follow-up on today's tasks will go on future to-do lists, as will those tasks yet to be completed.

- Fit in new tasks. Suppose you get another assignment crossing your desk midmorning. Determine its priority, and file it accordingly. If you are in doubt, ask the boss.

- Know why you're calling. Phone calls that need to be made should list name, phone number, and the reason for the call. Then, you can avoid the momentary blank that can occur when you have lots of calls to make.

- Use your lists as a diary. If you keep these lists organized, you can refer to any date and see when the task was completed, what type of follow-through occurred, and any other details about the assignment. This can be handy when it comes time to revamp your job description.

A to-do list is the single most effective time-management tool you have. You don't have to spend time or brainpower trying to remember what comes next. It's written out for you. Mark down any tasks delegated to others to make follow-up easy and to spot problems quickly. Your to-do list can save you time, energy, and your sanity. It's no wonder that many office professionals make much ado about to-do lists.

YES, YOU CAN STOP PROCRASTINATING!

Procrastination is a self-defeating behavior pattern that you *can* learn to change, says Lester R. Bittel, author of *Right on Time! The Complete Guide for Time-Pressured Managers* (McGraw-Hill). Here are a few of Bittel's suggestions for making that change:

- Make a list of the reasons why you want to stop procrastinating. Review it often.

- Put a stop to habits or routines associated with your procrastination. For instance, stop drinking coffee and reading the newspaper as a way of putting off certain distasteful tasks. Reward yourself each time you win the war with your desire to put things off.

- Don't allow any exceptions to your new habit at first. This is essential for a long-term behavior change.

- Develop momentum to get yourself going on a difficult task you keep putting off. Spend 15 to 30 minutes on something you don't mind doing and then tackle the tough stuff. Set an alarm that will tell you when your "getting started" period is over.

Now, get busy!

INTERRUPTIONS CUT INTO THE BOTTOM LINE

Work interruptions can decrease productivity and contribute to on-the-job stress. Regina Zekis, corporate trainer and vice president of R.B. Service Group, in Arlington Heights, Illinois, offers six tips for minimizing interruptions:

1. **If possible, adjust your work area so that you are not a target for interruptions.**(But don't try these tactics if your job involves contact with customers!) Here's how:

   a. Make it difficult for people to make eye contact with you. Turn your desk around if you're located in an area where people can easily see your face.

   b. Position your desk so it's not visible from any doorway. If you're out of their line of sight, people won't be so inclined to drop by.

   c. Make it impossible for people to sit down and talk. Stack books on any chairs in your workstation.

2. **Be brief and direct.** Says Zekis: "Asking, 'How can I help you?' encourages a visitor to focus on the specific reason why he or she wants to talk with you."

ACTION IDEA

Just how serious is your problem with interruptions? Try this: For the next few days, keep a log of all interruptions. Then, evaluate your findings. What interruptions could have been avoided? Who, among your colleagues or coworkers, interrupts you most often? Sit down with the worst offenders and work out a plan for cutting back on the interruptions.

a. Stand during conversations to convey the message that you don't have time for small talk.

b. And stand during telephone conversations as well. "Standing helps you feel in control, which, in turn, helps you focus on the gist of the conversation and limit its length," says Zekis.

c. If the conversation requires more than 10 minutes, suggest a meeting at a later time.

3. **Limit socializing to the proper time and place.** "A five-minute chat can easily go on for half an hour," Zekis notes. "To avoid this, when the talk is obviously turning social, suggest that you and your visitor meet for coffee or lunch break to 'catch up.'" Then, it doesn't seem as if you're giving the person a brush-off.

4. **Model the behavior you desire of others.** If you don't want peers to interrupt you without good reason, don't do it to them.

5. **Control phone time.** A few ideas for using the phone efficiently:

a. Don't set yourself up for telephone tag. When you reach someone's machine or voice mail, Zekis advises, leave a detailed message explaining what you want. The other person can then gather the information before calling you back and leave it in a message to you on your machine or voice mail.

b. Return telephone calls in "batches," rather than interrupt your work several times each day to make individual calls.

c. Make your calls as brief as possible by having all of the information you need right in front of you before picking up the telephone. Take a few seconds to collect your thoughts before you call.

6. **Organize your work.** Group similar tasks and do them at set times, filing for 30 minutes on Tuesday and Friday afternoons, for example.

'SORRY, GOTTA GO!'

Some people like to talk. And talk. And talk. But who has time to spend chit-chatting? To get more control over the time you spend on a call, try this: Before placing a call, set a conservative time limit and stick to it, suggest consultants Jonathan and Susan Clark. Measure the call yourself with something as simple as an egg timer or a watch that shows seconds.

Develop a set of verbal gestures to sign off on time, they advise. The easiest (and most polite) phrases are those that indicate your concern over the other person's time rather than your own. Phrases the authors like include:

- "I really need to let you get back to work."
- "I've probably tied up your time long enough, so . . ."
- "You probably have a lot of important things to do."

You can also refer to the simple fact that the conversation is ending: "Before we hang up, I have just one more question."

To be sure there are no hard feelings, "this is also a wonderful time to 'smile' and ask a question," suggest the Clarks. For example: "(Smile!) Is there anything else we need to discuss? No? Great!"

SOME MINUTES SAVE HOURS

Certain minutes can save you precious hours during the workday, depending on how you use them. And some minutes that seem like time-wasters when you're in a hurry are really time savers. Those include the minutes you use the telephone to:

1. Verify information. Get it right the first time. Otherwise, you're likely to be going in the wrong direction.
2. Explain. Taking a few minutes to keep a customer informed can prevent confusion down the line.
3. Recheck your own work. Even if you know it's perfect, double-check. You may be surprised.
4. Elicit feedback. Get a clear understanding of what the caller wants. Reiterate what you understood from the conversation. If there is any misunderstanding, it will be immediately corrected.

PUNCTUALITY ISN'T JUST ABOUT TIME MANAGEMENT

Everyone has arrived late at work at some time. Unforeseen events can prevent us from getting where we have to be. Most bosses make allowances for this, as long as the system is not abused.

But punctuality isn't just a time management problem. Some people make the mistake of thinking that time and punctuality are not important factors in the workplace. They justify their actions by minimizing the importance of them, saying that they just are not "morning people," or talking as if punctuality were just physically impossible for them.

In reality, these punctuality-impaired people tarnish their professional images, alienate coworkers, and severely limit their chances for career advancement. Whether stated or not, time is a high priority in most business cultures. These cultures expect others to honor that. A respect for punctuality says a lot about how you view work in general and your job in particular.

Chronic tardiness can send a message to others that you don't particularly care about your job, the company, or your coworkers. It says that

ACTION IDEA

Schedule a "productivity hour" for each day at work or at home. Shut the door, refuse telephone calls, and concentrate on one special task.

It takes tenacity and concentration to overcome ingrained habits like procrastination, but you can do it. There is great satisfaction in seeing a project through from start to finish. Let yourself enjoy that special feeling of achievement.

you're not interested in or willing to perform your assigned work, and that you are not organized. In reality, punctuality is a matter of choice. For example, if you thought that meeting with the boss at the starting time meant you were to receive a bonus check, you would probably make every effort to get there on the dot.

Tardiness can damage relationships with coworkers by breeding resentment. Why? Others probably resent the fact that you think the rules don't apply to you. You're not a team player. When coworkers suspect a double standard is operating, they have every right to be annoyed.

Those who get ahead know the value of time. They have a respect for the corporate work ethic. If the boss hasn't spoken to those who are habitually late, don't assume that he or she just doesn't notice. Their habits could come back to haunt them later.

To promote an employee, managers must know they can count on him or her. Typically, they do not reward those who scoff at the corporate system. If you want your coworkers to respect you, reevaluate your current time-management habits before this punctuality issue defeats you.

OVERTIME DEMANDS LIFESTYLE ADJUSTMENTS

In some sectors, people are finding it necessary to put in more overtime than ever before. This push is often the result of corporate downsizing or quality initiatives. Overtime puts many pressures on workers' free time. Although the money is often good, there are personal costs to consider, including increased stress and time-management problems. For example, when the employees at the Susquehanna Steam Electric Station were tasked with starting up a plant in northeastern Pennsylvania, 100-hour workweeks were common. To help them better manage their time, they developed a list of guidelines.

You, too, can benefit from these tips when your workload demands extra attention:

- Budget your free time. The period between when you leave work and when you go to sleep is your only source of flexible time. Determine the amount of time you spend on day-to-day responsibilities such as getting your child to and from day care, grocery shopping, housekeeping, and the like. Budget less time for these tasks, so that you can have time to yourself. For example, consider negotiating with other parents to alternate trips to day care. Don't forget to schedule time to just relax.

- Learn to say no. Explain to friends and family seeking favors that now is not the time for you to sponsor new projects or help with any old ones. Take the time to explain to children why your time is limited right now. If you don't manage your time, others will.

- Rest adequately. Get a solid, eight-hour block of sleep, if you can. Don't overexert yourself at home so that you are too tired to remain alert at work. Staying wide awake during an extended workday requires concentration. When deprived of sleep, your ability to concentrate tends to suffer. In a plant where there is heavy equipment and other areas of potential danger, this could be hazardous to you and your coworkers.

• Maintain your energy level. Energy maintenance is critical to feeling alert. A daily, 15-minute workout of walking, running, or simple calisthenics will greatly increase your energy level. Foods high in fat will slow you down and make you feel sluggish. Try a diet high in carbohydrates and low in fats. Increase your intake of vegetables, fresh fruits, broiled chicken and fish, and salads with low-fat dressings. The lighter diet will give you more energy, allow you to sleep better, and make you feel better about yourself.

• Renew yourself. Manage your time and energy during your company's busy time. Don't let negative thoughts affect your personal well-being. Most people feel good when they know they did a good job. Think positively about how your overtime income will aid your family and personal goals. If extra income isn't part of the picture, focus on how your career is likely to benefit from this display of dedication and hard work.

Like the folks at the Susquehanna Steam Electric Station, you'll feel rewarded for your hard work. And, during this crunch period, you just might learn to better manage your time.

QUICK TIPS

- **Turn up the radio?** So you think peace and quiet make you more productive at work? Not always, according to a workplace survey by Accountemps on Call. More than half of those surveyed say they perform better in a busy environment. Only 40 percent say their performance is better when working in a quiet atmosphere.

- **Save your time and mine.** Ask customers when is the best time for calling them. You'll show that you're considerate of their time and you'll save yourself from having to make so many callbacks.

- **Respect coworkers' time.** If you're running a meeting, make sure it starts on time even if some attendees are late. Show respect for those who are on time and let latecomers know the world goes on without them. They'll make more effort next time.

- **Keep meetings on track.** Assign one person at your next meeting to track interruptions that take the team away from the meeting goal or agenda.

- **Nix the personal calls.** Employees who use the company phone for personal calls often say they do so because they might forget to make their calls later. Fight that temptation by keeping a personal notepad near your desk phone. Use it to write down the calls you want to make when you get home.

- **Stop phone call waste.** Company executives waste at least one month each year on unnecessary or unproductive phone calls, according to a survey by Motivational Systems, a management development firm. To save time, the firm advises: plan before dialing, conclude conversations decisively, and skip non-vital calls.

QUIZ

Is Paper Pile-Up Doing You In?

"Sometimes, I get so disorganized at work. Not only is this reducing my efficiency, but it is threatening some of my work relationships. I get the feeling that others think they cannot count on me. What can I do?"

— *A.Y.D., Addison, Illinois*

Don't get discouraged. The more upset and self-conscious you get about your situation, the worse it will get. Organization can be learned. Odette Pollar, author of *Organizing Your Workspace* (Crisp Publications), says, "People aren't born organized. There's no genetic predisposition toward labeling and classifying systems. Organizing is a skill that's easy to learn." Use the following quiz to evaluate your organizational skills. It was adapted from one in Pollar's book and another developed by Stephanie Culp, author of *Conquering the Paper Pile-Up* (Writer's Digest Books).

	YES	NO
1. Do you have numerous scraps of paper and self-stick notes with information scribbled on them?	____	____
2. Must you spend big chunks of time when you need to locate certain information?	____	____
3. Do your coworkers have trouble finding materials that you supposedly filed?	____	____
4. Are you reluctant to throw any papers away because you might need them someday?	____	____
5. Are there items in your in-box that seem to have found a permanent home there?	____	____
6. Do you keep piles of paper and files around your office without the vaguest idea of what they actually contain?	____	____
7. Do you often misplace documents on your desk?	____	____
8. Do you accumulate periodicals because you can't find the time to read them?	____	____
9. Do you tell people not to touch anything in your work area because you know where everything is?	____	____
10. Are you often surprised to find materials in a certain spot because they're not where you thought they'd be?	____	____

TOTAL NUMBER OF YES ANSWERS: _____

Are you a victim of paper pile-up? If you were totally organized, you'd have tallied zero Yes answers. The more Yes answers you scored, the less organized you are. It might be a good time for you to clean house and get a fresh start. Use these questions as a guide to getting your workspace back in order before you make a fatal mistake.

YOUR CAREER SURVIVAL TOOL KIT TAKE-AWAY
The 3rd tool

Conquering time management

For the average person, 50 to 90 percent of time is taken up by seven or eight activities each day. That may include such time-users as telephone calls, requests from coworkers, meetings, informal chats over coffee, and mail. None of those areas should be outright ignored. But spending so much time on those activities leaves little time for looking at the big picture, or for being creative, or just relaxing. The secret to successful time management is to first uncover those seven or eight ways you're spending most of your time, and then finding ways to free up some time from each category. Trimming a little time from each area can add up to a significant amount of time that you can put to good use elsewhere. When you're known as someone who has conquered time management, you increase your value to your current employer and build your long-term career security. Coworkers and supervisors will enjoy working with you because you show respect for their time as well as your own. Time may not stop for anyone, but time management can be a valuable asset to your Career Survival Tool Kit.

WHAT YOU CAN DO

- **Keep a daily to-do list.** On a piece of paper, list the items you intend to do that day. List the large and small things that need doing. Set priorities for each item on your list. Put an A by the two or three items that are most important, a B beside the next most important, and a C beside the least important. Focus on the A's this morning and work through all the B's you can by the end of the day. Resist doing C's and don't do any B's until your A list is complete.

- **Spend less time in crisis mode.** "Think twice before leaving an important task in favor of one that shouts louder," suggest Sam Deep and Lyle Sussman in *Smart Moves for People in Charge* (Addison Wesley). "Many crises don't deserve the attention we give them."

- **Three times each day, ask yourself, "Is this the best use of my time?"** When the answer is no, switch to more meaningful work.

- **Find a way technology can help.** Routine tasks like record keeping can often be completed much more quickly on the computer.

- **Reserve one hour each day for yourself.** Managing time effectively doesn't mean just cramming in all the work you can. It should mean finding more time for the activities you enjoy.

INDEX

S

T

THE CUSTOMER SERVICE REP'S
SURVIVAL GUIDE SERIES FROM DARTNELL

Have you ever thought how many businesses lose money because customer service reps are not properly versed in the fine art of dealing with people? *The Customer Service Rep's Survival Guide Series* is a quick and easy way to motivate and train customer service reps to perform their best!

Completely unpretentious, the guides are written and illustrated for quick and easy reading. The guides also have a serious message — to teach your customer service team practical tips, inspiration, and insights into human nature. Whether they work with two customers a day or 200; your reps will improve the relationship your company has with all its customers. And that adds up to increased sales.

TOUGH CUSTOMERS:
How to Keep them Smiling ... and Yourself Sane!

This book teaches the front line how to deal with tough customers. Specifically, problem solving and handling unique situations as they arise. Topics include:

- Dealing with difficult customers, including keeping cool under pressure.
- Problem prevention — is the customer always right?
- Serving customers according to needs, giving special care to older customers, children, and disabled customers.

230 pages; paperback; $13.95; Book Code: 8124

STANDOUT SERVICE
Talk Straight, Think Positive, and Smile!

The first volume is the basics, emphasizing attitude and courtesy to customers. Topics include:

- What is customer service?
- Recognizing customers' needs and providing timely service

- How technology can improve your skills — including using the fax machine and voice mail.

227 pages; paperback; $13.95; Book Code: 8123

THE EXTRA MILE:
Building Profitable
Customer Relations Every Time

This book is designed to show how to go the extra distance with every customer encounter:

- Evaluating customer needs through critical questioning.
- Transforming the order taker into the customer sales rep through cross-selling and building repeat business.
- Encouraging a companywide commitment to service and improving lines of communication.

237 pages; paperback; $13.95; Book Code: 8122

TELEPHONE TERRIFIC!
Facts, Fun, and
103 Practical Tips
for Phone Success

Whether you're a customer service rep, salesperson, secretary, receptionist, telemarketer, or just anyone who conducts business over the phone, **TELEPHONE TERRIFIC!** will help you to brush up on the basics; to handle tricky situations; to think on your feet (and on the phone); and, through humorous and historical looks at telephones and the people who use them, to take the tough times less seriously.

- More than 100 helpful Quick Tips — helpful ideas and suggestions for better communication skills — throughout the book.
- Close-up interviews with telephone pros — take a stroll through the nostalgic past; learn how the pros keep up with technology; define customer satisfaction, and more.
- Test you skills — each chapter ends with a quiz so you can test and sharpen your skills.

172 pages; paperback; $10.95; Book Code: 8492